CYC
T
HEBR
WAY

A comprehensive guide for cyclists with maps, routes and listings

By The Offcomers

FFCOMERS

Published by The Offcomers

First edition published in 2016
Second edition published in 2017
Reprinted 2018

This edition uses maps created with Memory-Map
© Crown copyright and database rights
 2017 Ordnance Survey 100034184

The Offcomers is the trading name of Janet Moss and Pete Martin.

Photos are all taken by the Offcomers.

This book was researched and written by the Offcomers.

Thanks are due to countless people in the Outer Hebrides and other friends and colleagues who have given time, support and encouragement for this project.

Printed in the UK by Badger Press, Bowness on Windermere, Cumbria.

ISBN 978-0-9956770-2-9

www.theoffcomers.co.uk
info@theoffcomers.co.uk

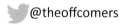 @theoffcomers

 facebook.com/theoffcomers

Cycling the Hebridean Way

CONTENTS

About this guide and the Hebridean Way

This book is a guide to cycling along the chain of the Outer Hebridean islands, on the 180-mile (292km) route known as the Hebridean Way. It runs from the southernmost permanently inhabited island (Vatersay) to the northernmost tip of the most northerly (The Butt of Lewis).

Developed and signed by Sustrans as National Cycle Network Route 780, the Hebridean Way was officially opened in March 2016, when around-the-world cyclist Mark Beaumont completed it within 24 hours. If you want to do it as quickly as possible, that's the time to beat. He hired a RIB (Rigid Inflatable Boat) to get him across the two sea crossings, but even using ferries you could do it within a day if you really put your mind to it.

But if you did that, you would miss much of what the islands have to offer. Part of their attraction is that the way of life is, or appears to be, slower than that many of us lead. One feels closer to the rocks, wind, waves, birds and flowers. People in the islands are often very friendly and willing to chat. Many of the best bits, and some of the best cycling routes, are off the main route up the spine of the islands. We have made suggestions for detours and walks. Do them. Find others. Visit sites along the way. You will have a good time. You will learn about the culture, history, natural history and landscape, discover the interesting and unexpected. Have that conversation. Take time: your journey and holiday will be more memorable for doing a bit of exploring.

Our aim has been to produce a guide that is easy to use, accurate and informative. We cannot include all the information that you might discover you want, but we hope to be able to signpost you so that you do not become lost; to give you indications of things that are of interest; prompts to make you think and find out more; and to provide enough information about accommodation and supplies.

We are keen cyclists and lovers of the Hebrides. We have visited the islands many times. But we are not superhuman 100-mile-a-day athletes. We are prone to aches, pains, lethargy and laziness. We are easily distracted by ruins, wildlife and the chance of a good walk. We like decent lunches and know what it is that unites cyclists: cake stops!

Using this guide

We have designed the book so it fits into our handlebar bags. It is divided into three parts:

1. Introductory sections about the route, cycling in the Outer Hebrides, history, information about the landscape.

2. The described route: a detailed guide, split into 5 sections, including Ordnance Survey maps, with references to all listings (see below) and the route clearly marked. We have written a description of what you can expect to find, together with information about some sights along the way, suggested detours you can take on your bike and some walks.

3. The listings. At the back of the book is a list of accommodation, cafes, shops and bike repair/ hire outlets, cross referenced to the maps.

You can, of course, cycle the route in either direction, but we have written it as though you are cycling from south to north. That way, the prevailing wind is behind you, though there is no guarantee that the actual winds will be prevailing. Where we are aware that things are different or difficult if you are heading the other way, we have given that information.

Each individual route section is presented in a consistent way including:
• Overview map showing the route and how we have divided the sections up
• 1:50,000 scale maps: the route goes from A to B and is marked in black
  Sometimes , where the map is over two pages, the direction of travel is marked with arrows for clarity
• The map key is inside the back cover. Places for refreshments and provisions are marked, as are detours (in orange)
• Gradient profile (based on contours from the map)
• Written route information (and difficulties if there are any)
• Places of interest (both on the route and nearby)

We have tried to include all the places where you could stay or eat or drink along the way. At the time of visiting (spring 2017) they were all there. Entry in this book does not infer any recommendation and no opinion is offered on the adequacy of anything mentioned. Things may have changed since we were there: facilities open and shut at a surprisingly fast rate. Please let us know if you find anything new (or closed) and we will update via our website. Please contact us direct for any known changes to our listings before you make your trip.

USE PASSING PLACES TO PERMIT OVERTAKING

Practicalities- Cycling the Route

The Hebridean Way follows roads, often A roads, though these are generally quiet. Some of the surfaces are far from smooth, and many are single track with passing places. There are hills, but nothing more than 180m/600ft of ascent/ descent at any one time, and they are generally not steep. You do not need to take a mountain bike: a road bike will be fine. The most important things are that you are comfortable with your bike, that it fits you well, and that you can ride it comfortably for as long as you need.

If you are not used to single track roads with passing places, it is worth reading this paragraph. Give way to vehicles coming towards you (especially) if they are on business or coming uphill. Give way by pulling in to the passing place if it is on your side of the road, or stopping opposite the passing place if it is on the other. Allow vehicles coming along behind you to overtake. You may think this will not apply as there is room and time for vehicles to overtake you. But some roads are very narrow and you will obstruct the vehicles behind you at some point. Let them pass! You may of course be able to overtake some road users: a tractor carrying peats once pulled in to allow a car towing a trailer of lobster pots to pass which in turn stopped to allow me to get ahead!

There are very few specific bike shops/ repairers along the island chain, and fewer on the route itself. So, you should aim to be self-sufficient with maintenance. On the other hand, if things go wrong, there are people who can help (see our listings), and almost every crofter will have a tool set and a basic knowledge of how to fix things...

Carry your belongings in a way that you are comfortable with. We would recommend paniers fixed to the bike, rather than a rucsac. Make sure the bags are waterproof as Hebridean rain, even when it doesn't seem to be that heavy, has a knack of getting into the most unlikely nooks and crannies. Take windproof and waterproof clothing to deal with the weather.

Many parts of the Outer Hebrides have very few facilities, so it's a good idea to always carry some basic rations, even if you never have to use them. From Benbecula northwards, almost every facility is shut on Sundays.

SUNDAY USAGE
IT WOULD BE APPRECIATED IF MEMBERS
OF THE PUBLIC WOULD RESPECT THE
WISHES OF THE COMMUNITY BY REFRAINING
FROM USING THE PLAYPARK ON THE
LORD'S DAY

SCALPAY PLAY AR
PLEASE NOTE,
CHILDREN SHOULD BE OUT
PLAY AREA EACH NIGHT BY 9.
CLOSED ON SUNDAY

Practicalities- Beds and Cake

Where to stay? A big question. Personal preference, finance, practicality and the desire to keep the load to a minimum come into play. The distances involved, and lack of provision in some areas, may dictate your choice. To pre-book or not? You may need certainty at busy times. But the weather may encourage you to go further, or make you want to sit out a day. And that cannot be planned for.

Overnight stays often provide a great opportunity to interact with local people: this is where you will find out about the culture and how lovely many Hebrideans are.

Camping: There are relatively few commercial campsites on the islands, but some are gorgeous, with the best views in the world from your tent door. The long tradition of wild camping is reinforced by the Scottish Outdoor Access Code. But be responsible: limit stays to two or three nights in any one place, don't camp in enclosed fields of crops or livestock and keep well away from buildings, roads or historic structures. If you wish to camp close to a house or building, seek the owner's permission. Take away all your litter, remove all traces of your tent pitch and any open fire and don't cause any pollution. Obviously, we cannot say where the best places to wild camp are. Be careful how you leave your pitch, as others will have to deal with any mess (physical or metaphorical) you leave.
The Community Trusts are interested in accommodation for campers: they have developed camper van hook-up sites and encouraged camping alongside laybys (for a fee) in Harris.

Hostels: There are now no Scottish Youth Hostel Association (SYHA) hostels in the islands, but there are three run by the Gatliff Hebridean Hostels Trust (a charity dedicated to running hostels, in partnership with islanders) at Howmore (South Uist); Berneray, and Rhenigidale (Harris). There are also other hostel providers, some of whom offer outdoor activities: see listings for details.

Hotels and B&Bs: These may, or may not, be cycle friendly. When booking, it is worth enquiring about dry places to keep your bike etc.

Eating: Our policy on cake is to both have it and eat it. Often. Cyclists must keep their fuel levels topped up to avoid the bonk. There are many places along the Hebridean Way to obtain tea and fuel: community centres and galleries often provide refreshments. There are far fewer pubs/ restaurants and few shops selling food. Our directory and maps identify these. Sundays in the islands north of Benbecula, when almost everything will be shut, are particularly difficult. Plan ahead to deal with Sundays.

The Big Issue- Getting there and back

The Hebridean Way is a one-way route, so you will have to get home afterwards. This will involve logistical planning: there are far too many transport access options and possibilities for us to list them all.

Getting to/ from Vatersay:

Ferry from Oban (rail link) to Castlebay (operated by Caledonian MacBrayne www.calmac.co.uk 0800 066 5000): 4 hr 45 mins crossing time. Daily ferries, tending (in summer) to leave Oban early afternoon, arriving at Castlebay early evening. Leaving Castlebay early morning, getting to Oban at lunchtime.

Flights to Barra airport are operated from Glasgow by Flybe, but do not take bicycles as the aircraft are too small to carry them.

Trains to Oban are operated by Scotrail (www.scotrail.co.uk).

There is free long term car parking at Longsdale and Lochavullin car parks in Oban.

Getting to/ from Stornoway:

Ferry from Ullapool (no rail link) to Stornoway: 2 ½ hour crossing time. Operated by Calmac (details as above). Two ferries a day (one on Sundays), leaving Stornoway early morning and afternoon, leaving Ullapool mid-morning and early evening.

The bike bus previously operated by D&E Coaches did not run in 2017. But Ticket to Ride (www.tickettoridehighlands.co.uk) can provide cycle transport. Scottish Citylink (www.citylink.co.uk) operate buses to Ullapool from Inverness and may take bikes: contact them for details of current situation. You may need a box or bag. Some people cycle to the train station at Garve (about 32 miles).

Flights go from Stornoway airport to Inverness, Aberdeen, Glasgow, Edinburgh and Benbecula (see www.hial.co.uk). Bikes can be carried: contact Flybe (www.flybe.com) for details.

Other possibilities:

Couriers such as Hebrides Haulage can take your bikes: www.hebrideshaulage.co.uk. Bespoke and Bike Hebrides (see listings) can transport you and your bike.

Alternatively, you could consider one of the bike hire packages offered by firms such as Hebridean Hopscotch: www.hebrideanhopscotch.com.

Intermediate ferries (operated by Calmac) from Tarbert or Lochmaddy to Uig on Skye, or Lochboisdale to Mallaig may also be worth considering.

Or you might take the "easy" way out of the logistical nightmare, by extending your trip and cycling back to the start!

More Practicalities

Ferries between the islands: The ferries from Ardmhor on Barra to Eriskay, and from Berneray to Leverburgh on Harris are both operated by Caledonian MacBrayne: www.calmac.co.uk. At the time of writing, bicycles travel for free. The fares are £2.95 per adult on the Sound of Barra ferry (five crossings per day) and £3.45 on the Sound of Harris (four crossings per day, three on Sundays). Booking may be necessary at busy times, and limited numbers of bikes can be carried. Crossings can be affected by the weather and tide conditions. Check for alterations!

Buses: At the time of writing, buses on Lewis and Harris may take bicycles at the driver's discretion. Buses on other islands do not take bikes. Timetables can be found at: www.cne-siar.gov.uk/travel/busservice.

Taxis: There are a number of taxi companies on the islands and also some bike hire operators who will provide transport if booked.

Language: The Gaelic language is an important part of the Outer Hebrides' identity: more than half the residents are Gaelic speakers. Education is provided in Gaelic medium: children are taught in the local language. The least "Gaelic speaking area" is Stornoway. But don't worry: islanders will always speak to you in English and the "rules" of hospitality mean that they will conduct any conversation when you are present in English! Road signs in most of the islands are in both English and Gaelic in many areas, and some attractions proudly display their Gaelic heritage in their names – such as the An Lanntair centre in Stornoway or the Taigh Chearsabhagh museum and arts centre in Lochmaddy. For those of us who do not speak Celtic languages, the pronunciation of written Gaelic will be confusing, though a little work beforehand can make it easier and it will not be long before you are picking up the common elements to many place names (if you know a little Welsh, things may begin to make sense more quickly). We have used a mixture of Gaelic/ English place names, generally what is on the OS map.

Money: Many island businesses are cash only businesses, and don't take card payments. Cash points (ATMs) are relatively few and far between, so it may be worth your while stocking up on cash before heading to the islands.

Mobile Phones/ Internet: Signals can be erratic, subject not just to line of sight problems, but also to the weather. Be prepared to be uncontactable at times. Some tourist businesses have Wi-Fi. This may, or may not, be strong enough for your needs. Tourist information offices and Calmac ferries and terminals also have free Wi-Fi. You will not be the first person to hang around an empty ferry terminal surfing the signal.

Hebridean Landscapes

In some ways, the Outer Hebrides landscape is simple: it is almost all made up of the same rock; Lewisian gneiss. Up to 2.9 billion years old, this is the oldest rock in Britain, and some of the oldest in the world. Exposures show how it has been contorted and twisted by deep pressures and high heats over an unimaginable length of time. It is a very resistant rock and deeply impermeable: hence the build-up of water to form lochs and bogs. The only rocks on the islands that are not Lewisian gneiss are on the east coast of Lewis and the Point peninsular.

Today's landscape has been hugely affected by the very recent (in geological terms) glacial and post glacial activity. Ice sheets covered the islands several times in the past couple of million years: hills like Clisham sometimes protruded as what are called "nunataks", subject to huge frost shattering processes. The ice wore away and smoothed much of the rock. It transported boulders around, having plucked them from their beds. It ground out big fjords like Loch Seaforth, and small hollows almost everywhere. When the ice melted, it dumped debris all over the place and the meltwaters carved channels like Glen Valtos in Uig.

At the end of the last ice age, 11000 or so years ago, the islands were linked together. Sea levels rose, and the land was divided. Vegetation (including trees) colonised. Soils developed. But, around 7000 years ago, the climate became a little cooler and wetter. The impermeable gneiss prevented water from running off. It collected in the glacial hollows and stopped the plant matter from rotting down. The resulting, partially decayed, material is the peat that blankets the landscape today.

Meanwhile, under the sea to the west, the ice sheets had dumped large amounts of glacial debris. Mixed by ocean currents with the remains of crushed shells from deeper water marine life, this calcareous sand was gradually swept eastwards and blown ashore. The shell sand (as it is called) forms the beaches, dunes, and what is called the machair, the flower-rich sandy plain that follows the west coast of the islands.

The result of all these process is an intricate landscape of rock and water, sand and grassland and bog. In just a short distance the views, the nature and the potential for human activity changes dramatically. A variety that helps make the Outer Hebrides so fascinating.

A very brief human history

People arrived at the end of the ice age: peat samples suggest they burnt the forest cover, Mesolithic sites provide evidence of stone tools. Stones at Callanish and elsewhere provide striking indications of a rich early history. The varied Iron Age roundhouses (e.g. Carloway broch and at Bosta on Great Bernera) reflect different cultural needs and influences.

The Norse (Vikings) arrived in the 9th century: their legacy is in many place names. Sumarlidi, the summer raider, seized control in the twelfth century. His sons (Donald and Dougall) divided territory between them, founding the clans of Macdonald and MacDougall. After the 1262 Battle of Largs, Norway sold the Hebrides to Scotland: the Islay based Lords of the Isles, Clan Donald, controlled them. As their power waned after 1500, more local clan chiefs gained importance: MacNeil (Barra), Ranald (South Uist), MacLeod (Harris and Lewis).

Change to modern ways came slowly: in 1675 MacNeil of Barra greeted the King's messenger with a volley of shots. Some island lairds supported the Jacobite rebellions of 1715 and 1745. Prince Charlie's flight through the Hebrides is the stuff of romantic legend. But things changed after the '45: landlords, when they regained their lands, sought to maximise their income.

Across the Highlands, in the 1780s and 90s, the clearances began. But the Hebrides boomed as seaweed was burnt: kelp made chemicals for industry. The surge in profits went to the landlord, but the population swelled. And then came the crash. Islands were sold. New owners thought sheep farming more profitable than people. Evictions followed. Potato blight struck. The hardship was immense. Thousands left for the mainland and Canada: many voluntarily, some forcibly.

The 1886 Crofting Act gave those with a croft some security of tenure, but for those without land the act did nothing. Raids by the landless took place sporadically: some crofts were allocated. WW1 recruiting posters promised land for the heroes, but hundreds of returning servicemen died when the Iolaire sank off Stornoway on New Year's morning 1919.

Islands were at the mercy of their landowners. Lady Cathcart, owner of Barra and South Uist, is thought to have visited once in 58 years. Soap magnate Lord Leverhulme bought Lewis in 1918 and Harris a year later, aiming to create an industrialised fishery supplying his MacFisheries shops. But islanders wanted their own crofts and to fish part-time. Leverhulme sold Lewis in 1923, and died before his plans could come to fruition in Harris. The islands returned to varied landownership. But in recent years, community buy-outs have led to local people gaining ownership: how will this affect the Hebrides? Will young people always emigrate? Only time will tell.

Natural History

Naturalists find islands intriguing because of their more limited range of species and greater "inbreeding" than on the "mainland". The Outer Hebrides, on the edge of Europe, have interesting things turn up on planned migrations, or when they lose their way. A low density of human population (and low intensity agriculture) has helped things survive that have elsewhere become rare.

So, what does that mean for the passing cyclist? Firstly, you are really quite likely to see sea mammals: cetaceans (dolphins and porpoises) are very regularly seen from ferries; common or grey seals are in every bay; otters are on almost every stretch of coastline (best watched for at dusk).

The lack of mammalian predators means ground nesting birds, particularly waders, breed in comparatively large numbers. In season, you can expect to see or hear redshank, greenshank, oystercatcher, dunlin, snipe, lapwing, golden plover and curlew. There are good populations of birds of prey: perhaps the highest densities of golden and white tailed eagles in the UK, and good numbers of hen harrier and merlin too. The Bird of Prey Trail (http://www.visitouterhebrides.co.uk/see-and-do/nature/bird-of-prey-trail/locations) suggests places to visit. But other places are as good, if not better! Birds that have suffered with agricultural intensification elsewhere are found in good numbers: corncrakes have increased in the last 20 years or so with the RSPB's help, and corn buntings hold on.

The machair, being relatively lime-rich, fertile but not over-fertilised, and grazed, but not heavily, boasts magnificent displays of daisies, orchids and trefoils to name but a few. The number of species is not that high, but the effect can be dramatic. Insects flourish too: bumblebees, including some rare species, do well.

But the machair is at risk: global warming means sea levels may rise, and storm damage increase. Visitors and vehicles trample and erode. What we see is the result of a delicate balance. Wildlife is very vulnerable to disturbance from introduced animals like hedgehogs and mink: both have been the subject of eradication programmes. Alien plants like Gunnera can become rampant, excluding the more natural flora. There is an ever-present drive towards agricultural "improvement", but abandoning farming can also lead to species loss. And as for the plastic in the oceans...

In short, the Outer Hebrides are a naturalists' heaven. Keep your eyes open, because the more one looks, the more one sees...

Along the Way

Lazy beds
Traditional cultivation involved spreading seaweed on the ground and turning the soil over on top. Over the years a corrugated landscape of feannagan, lazybeds in English, developed (it must have been back-breaking work). Lazybeds are often seen in surprising places, and give clues to where people once lived.

Peat Cutting
Formed when plant material fails to break down in a cool, wet climate, Britain is well endowed with peat, and the Outer Hebrides especially so. The impermeable gneiss , and the innumerable hollows carved by the glaciers, have led to vast areas forming, and great depths: up to 6 metres in places on Lewis. For centuries, it has been the main source of fuel. Peat cuttings are allocated via a complicated system: you will see drying peats on the moor and stacks in gardens. You will smell the sweet reek from chimneys, even in high summer. Mmmmm…

Ruins
Archaeologists use some confusing terms, so here are some definitions:

Chambered cairn: A burial monument, probably Neolithic, where a sizeable stone chamber has had a heap of stones put over it.

Atlantic roundhouses: Several sorts of Iron Age round building are found in the Outer Hebrides: some simple (where people lived?) and some more complex (for ritual, defence, or as prestige dwellings?).

Wheelhouse: Iron Age (c 5000BC-500AD) roundhouses with the interior subdivided by radial stone wall "spokes". They appear to have been monumental in size, and may well not have been "houses".

Broch: Iron Age circular towers built of two concentric, windowless stone walls, with a living space in the middle. It is uncertain when and why they were built.

Dun: A generic term for an ancient or mediaeval fort.

Crannog: A partially or entirely artificial island built in water.

Jelly baby houses: Also called 'figure-of-eight' buildings because of their plan shape, built by late Pictish peoples (c500-800AD).

Blackhouse: A more recent rectangular building of double wall dry-stone walls packed with earth and thatched with turf or straw. Smoke escaped through the roof.

Along the Way

Midges
The West Coast of Scotland is renowned for its biting midges, small insects that can render a beautiful summer's evening hellish. The midges in the Outer Hebrides are generally not as bad as in notorious hotspots like Skye. But they can still be a problem on still, dull days and evenings: seek out wind and light to reduce the effects. There are many different repellents available and we suggest you carry a midge hat if camping.

Harris Tweed
Harris Tweed originates from the hard-wearing cloth made by islanders for centuries. The Countess of Dunmore, who owned Harris in the mid-19th century, realised the potential of the fabric and encouraged production, training and marketing (the orb symbol is taken from the Dunmore coat of arms). In order to gain the badge, a tweed has to be hand-woven by an islander at their home in the Outer Hebrides, finished in the islands and made from pure virgin wool dyed and spun in the Outer Hebrides. The Harris Tweed Act of 1993 established the Harris Tweed Authority to oversee the industry.
Traditionally, it has a well-organised and well-unionised workforce. In practice, very little weaving is done outside Harris and Lewis. In recent years there has been a resurgence in the popularity of the fabric and it has been used by many famous brands. As you travel the islands you will see weavers at work, mills at Shawbost and Carloway and various retail outlets.

Weather
Atlantic weather systems make their first contact with land in the Outer Hebrides. The ocean dominates: the islands are less cold in winter (and less hot in summer) than places further south and east. They are wetter than some places further south and east. And they are much windier than most places south and east. Stornoway has about twice as much rain as London, but only half the number of frosts. Summer temperatures are several degrees cooler. The sunniest months (and the driest ones) are April, May and June. The warmest are July and August. The months with lightest winds are July and August. It is the wind that dominates the climate, and sometimes life. Sandbags hold down the roofs of Lewis bus shelters, though many are four compartmented concrete structures designed so there is always a bit of shelter. Shipping containers are tied down on crofts. A visit to the islands will almost always involve experiencing some wind, but it is only the winter storms that necessitate the extreme safety measures.

Religion

The Outer Hebrides are a part of the UK where religion is at its most pervasive. The islands are split between the overwhelmingly Catholic Barra and South Uist, and the mainly Protestant North Uist, Harris and Lewis. Here, the Church of Scotland, the Free Presbyterian Church of Scotland and other groups have a massive cultural importance: Free Church ministers were important in resisting the Clearances and have contributed greatly to the preservation of the Gaelic language. The Sabbath is still strictly observed in many places. Whilst the swings in children's playgrounds may not be locked up these days, use of the swings in frowned upon, as is hanging out the washing (you may well see notices to that effect). Almost all shops, cafes and attractions will be shut. Whilst it is true that there has been some decline of religion as ferries now run on Sundays, it is best to be prepared and plan for the Sabbath.

A 2015 survey by the Legatum institute found that the Outer Hebrideans were the happiest people in the UK, and as result, their region was the fifth most "prosperous" despite average incomes being 135th in a list of 170 areas. Whether it is the religion, strong community, low crime rate, rich culture or pristine environment that makes this so, we will leave you to judge.

Some cultural adventures

Whisky Galore

Compton Mackenzie, who lived in Barra at the time, wrote a rather charming comic novel about the wartime sinking of the SS Politician and her cargo of whisky. Glossing over some of the incidents, the book was rather a success, and was filmed by Ealing Studios in 1949. A big hit in austerity Britain, it has remained a classic. A 2016 remake has, at the time of writing, received mixed reviews on its few outings.

Crowdie and Cream

Finlay Macdonald's memoirs of a childhood in Scarista on Harris between the wars, written by a true raconteur.

The Lewis Trilogy

Thriller writer Peter May's "Blackhouse", "Lewis Man" and "Chessmen" are set around the fictional township of Crobost, loosely based on Adabroc in Ness. His "Coffin Road" is set in Luskentyre. Whilst the characters are fictional, and the events (we hope) unlikely, much of the landscape and cultural detail is realistic. There is an online guide to Peter May's Outer Hebrides: http://www.visitouterhebrides.co.uk/see-and-do/culture-and-heritage/peter-may-lewis-trilogy

Section 1 Vatersay and Barra

Section 1 Vatersay and Barra

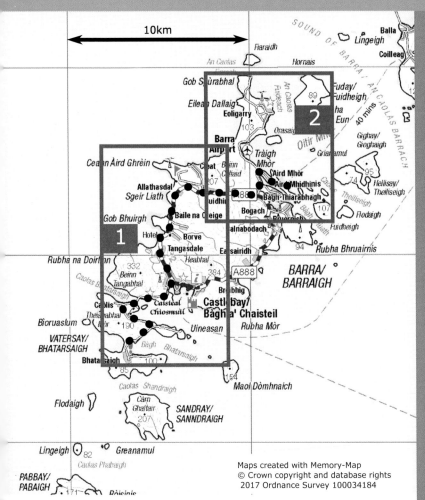

10km

Maps created with Memory-Map
© Crown copyright and database rights
2017 Ordnance Survey 100034184

Barra is sometimes described as the "Outer Hebrides in miniature", or as "Barradise". With sandy beaches, eagles soaring over the hills, a fascinating human history and lively culture, we wouldn't disagree with either statement. Together with the smaller island of Vatersay, it makes a great introduction to the Hebridean chain. Whilst you could cycle from Vatersay to the Eriskay Ferry in little over an hour, we recommend that you take your time and do some exploring: maybe complete the ring road round the island, or go up to the northern tip at Eoligarry. The view from Heabhal, Barra's highest point at 383m, is dramatic. It's a steep but straightforward climb from the col on the road east of Castlebay.

Barra, like many of the islands, has sandy beaches to the west and north, rougher and boggier ground to the east. Vatersay (from the Gaelic for "water island") is two low hills linked by a dune system. These days, it is the southernmost inhabited island in the Hebridean chain. But until last century, people lived on the islands further south: Berneray (Barrahead), Mingulay, Sandray and Pabbay. These can all be visited by hired boat from Castlebay: the dramatic coastal scenery, abundant wildlife and atmospheric islands can make for a memorable day trip (or longer).

Owned by Clan MacNeil from the time of the Norse, the islands were sold by the 41st Chief to Colonel Gordon of Cluny in 1838. The Colonel, who had previously been MP for Weymouth, and inherited his wealth from a West Indian merchant, also bought Benbecula, South Uist and Eriskay. He deemed the crofters redundant, and offered to turn the island into a penal colony. The government declined the offer, so the Colonel called in the police to help with the evictions. On Cluny's death, the islands were inherited in turn by his son, and by the son's second wife, Lady Cathcart.

The north of Barra was turned into one large sheep farm. Landless cottars raided that land. The Congested Districts Board bought land for crofts. In 1906, another group of landless men, from both Barra and Mingulay, raided Vatersay. The traditional tale was that the law allowed someone to stay if they built a house and lit a fire in it within 24 hours. So they built shelters and fires. They remained after being urged to leave. A visiting judge described them as "respectable" and recommended that the government buy the island. It refused, and the men were taken to court by Lady Cathcart. In June 1908, ten of the raiders were sentenced to two months in prison by an Edinburgh court. The case received huge publicity, the government quickly agreed to buy the land and the men were released a fortnight early. By August 1908 there were 34 families on the land: fifty-eight crofts were created when the Congested Districts Board completed the purchase the following year.

In 1937 the 45th Chief of Clan MacNeil (a Canadian) bought back the island of Barra. He began restoration of Kisimul Castle. The herring fishery, that had crammed the bay with boats early in the century, declined after WW1. In recent decades the bay has emptied. These days, most fish landing takes place at Northbay, where the Barratlantic fish processing business operates. In 2003, the MacNeils gave Barra to the Scottish government.

Vatersay had added difficulties because of the extra ferry crossing. Cattle were transported to market by ferry from Castlebay, but they first had to swim the 250 metres to Barra. In 1986 a prize bull called Bernie, uninsured despite belonging to the Department of Agriculture, drowned on the trip to the island. Three islanders were taken to court, but cleared of causing its death by drowning. The widespread publicity increased the pressure on the government. A causeway was built, which opened officially in 1991. These days around 90 people live on Vatersay (an increase since the causeway was built) and 1260 on Barra.

Vatersay and Barra

Castlebay

The name says it all really. The naturally sheltered bay is one of the finest harbours in the Outer Hebrides, and has long been commercially important. Reputedly, in the heyday of the herring fishery, one could walk from one side of the bay to the other across the moored boats!

Kisimul castle, perched on a rock surrounded by the sea, is a small, but perfect looking, fortress. Probably built in the fifteenth century, after the MacNeils had gained the island, it was abandoned in 1748 and sold in 1838. In 1937, Robert Lister MacNeil purchased it and began renovations. In 2001 it was leased to Historic Scotland for 1000 years for the annual sum of £1 and a bottle of whisky. Boats leave regularly from the pier opposite the post office. The views from the tower, and atmosphere, justify making the trip, even though the inside consists of more modern, empty buildings.

The village of Castlebay contains shops, cafes (try the scallop pakora from Café Kisimul!) and hotels. Most of the services on the island are to be found here.

Dualchas (map ref M)

A heritage centre, café and exhibitions explaining the island's history in a beautifully understated way.

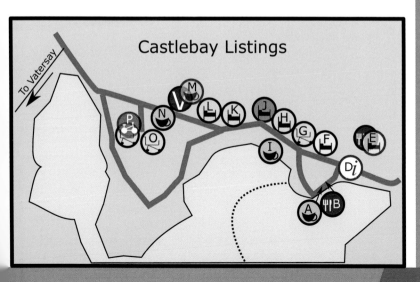

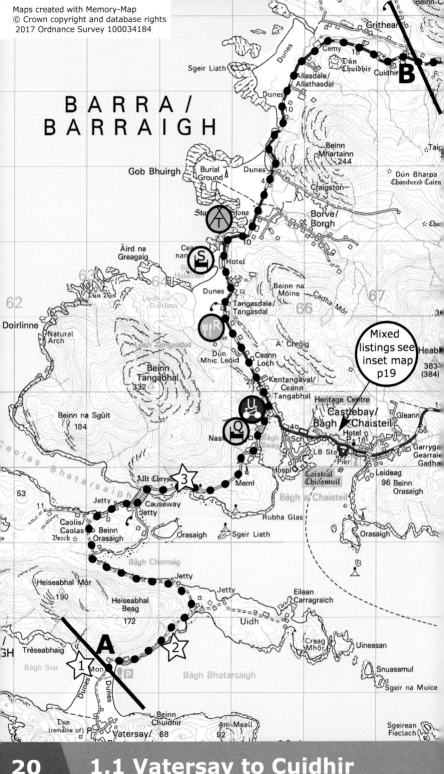

Section 1.1 Vatersay to Cuidhir
Distance 13.8 km (8.5 miles)
Total ascent 263m
Total descent 256m

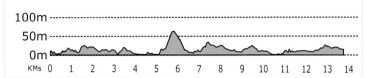

The Route

In all probability, you will arrive on the boat at Castlebay. Go up the slip road and turn left. Follow the road along past the Dualchas heritage centre on the right. At the Nasg turn off, turn left and head through the houses. Follow the road up to the war memorial and down to the causeway. Cross over to Vatersay and follow the main road round to the right. Go over the neck of land and around the first bay, passing the old ferry landing. Carry along the road, pass the left turn to Uidh, and then head along above Vatersay Bay. Pass the old school on your right, and then the community centre. In the dunes to the left is the sign marking the start of the Hebridean Way. If you want to cycle to the road end, it is a few hundred metres further on. If you want to dip your toe in the water, the east beach is probably best.

You can now start the Hebridean Way proper! Return the way you have come over the causeway and surprisingly steep (11.1%) hill. At the main road, turn left, climb another hill and descend to Tangasdale. Follow the main road along the coast past dunes, beaches and valleys leading into the Barra hills. The road turns inland, coming up to a church and houses.

Points of Interest

 Annie Jane Monument

In the dunes to the west of the road on Vatersay is the memorial to 350 emigrants who drowned when the Annie Jane sank on the way from Liverpool to Quebec in 1853. After storms carried away the topmasts, passengers pleaded with the captain to put back to Liverpool. He battened them below decks to prevent panic and mutiny.

 Catalina

In the burn to the east of the road on Vatersay are the remains of a Catalina flying boat that crashed into the island in 1944. Amazingly, six of those on board survived.

 Allt Chrysal

As you freewheel down towards the causeway, look out for Allt Easdail on the right, shown on maps as Allt Chrysal. It is not signed at the road, so is easy to miss. The site was discovered in 1990 when the roadbuilders were looking for a place for their cabins. The best spot had been used before! There is evidence of occupation from Neolithic times up to the nineteenth century: circular huts, an Iron Age house, a roundhouse, a wheelhouse, a burial cairn and a more modern blackhouse. Each occupation re-used materials from previous ones. There are also "lazy beds", where crops were grown. Go up to the site to see the information boards and historic remains.

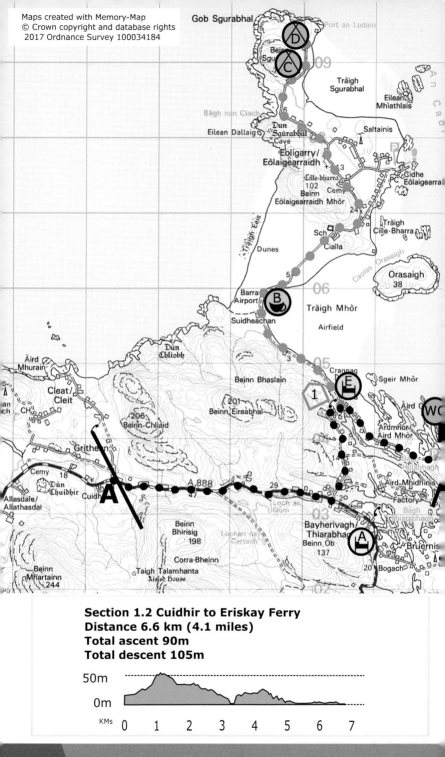

Maps created with Memory-Map
© Crown copyright and database rights
2017 Ordnance Survey 100034184

Section 1.2 Cuidhir to Eriskay Ferry
Distance 6.6 km (4.1 miles)
Total ascent 90m
Total descent 105m

The Route

Carry on along the main A888 over the pass. The road descends by Loch an Dun, then more steeply alongside a small woodland. Turn left at the junction in Northbay and head north. Pass the end of a sea loch, cross a neck of land and go round the head of a second loch. Take the second road on the right, signposted for Ardmhor and the ferry for Eriskay. This leads along the peninsular to the ferry jetty. There is a waiting room and toilet at the jetty; on occasions a café is open. There is also an attractive sculpture of two otters chasing a salmon.

The ferry (five crossings a day on weekdays in summer) to Eriskay takes about 40 minutes. It offers views of the beaches and islands in the sound of Barra. Common seals, gannets and terns are usually spotted. Both species of eagle, peregrine falcons and bottlenose dolphins may be seen if you are lucky.

Detour
North Barra

The cockle strand of Traigh Mhor hosts the island airport, the only one in the world where scheduled flights use a beach as a runway. Flight times vary with the tides. The planes used are Twin Otters.

The fertile north of the island, with its sandy beaches and machair croplands, was cleared in the 1820s and 1850s. The land was divided into farms. Eoligarry House, built by the 40th Chief around 1790, became the home of the notorious McGillivray family. They farmed the area for many years and were hard taskmasters, favouring Protestants over local Catholics. Following land raids in the Northbay area, the Congested Districts Board bought land at Eoligarry to create 58 crofts in 1901, and more at the end of WWI, though the McGillivrarys continued living in the grand house until 1939. The building was finally demolished in the 1970s. Modern council houses occupy some of the site today, as well as the Catholic church.

Nearby are the remains of the mediaeval Cille Bharra church and associated chapels, including a replica of the Kilbarr runic stone dating from before 1000AD. Compton Mackenzie, author of "Whisky Galore" and "The Monarch of the Glen", is buried in the churchyard.

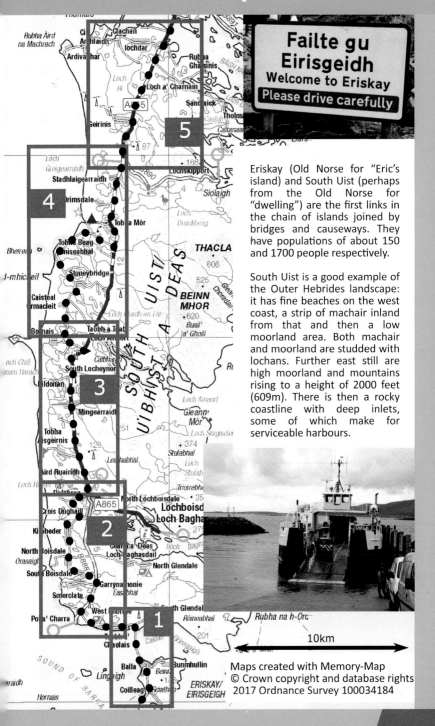

Failte gu Eirisgeidh
Welcome to Eriskay
Please drive carefully

Eriskay (Old Norse for "Eric's island") and South Uist (perhaps from the Old Norse for "dwelling") are the first links in the chain of islands joined by bridges and causeways. They have populations of about 150 and 1700 people respectively.

South Uist is a good example of the Outer Hebrides landscape: it has fine beaches on the west coast, a strip of machair inland from that and then a low moorland area. Both machair and moorland are studded with lochans. Further east still are high moorland and mountains rising to a height of 2000 feet (609m). There is then a rocky coastline with deep inlets, some of which make for serviceable harbours.

Maps created with Memory-Map
© Crown copyright and database rights
2017 Ordnance Survey 100034184

Human habitation is concentrated on the west coast machair plains, and the flat lands at the north and south. There is some population by the east coast inlets, these days primarily at Lochboisdale, the island's ferry terminal. Currently, this is served by boats from Mallaig, though until recently boats came from Oban. A recent major construction project has resulted in a new harbour and marina at Lochboisdale.

The island boasts many ancient monuments, some amongst the dunes and machair, others on the wilder, less inhabited east coast. The island was owned by Clan Ranald after the ending of the Lordship of the Isles, but following the collapse of the kelp industry in the early 19th Century, it was sold to Gordon Of Cluny. Clearances followed, and large scale emigration.

The museum at Kildonan illustrates many aspects of the history of the island and its peoples. Predominantly Catholic, it has a different atmosphere from the islands further north: shrines feature largely in the landscape you cycle through. It is an island with little in the way of "villages", as the population is mostly spread out across crofting townships. There are shops in Daliburgh, at Aird Mhor by the north causeway and Lochboisdale. The Hebridean Way doesn't visit the latter (it's probably not worth a detour). The traditional Gaelic culture is strong, illustrated by the summer music schools and Gaelic activities.

In 2006, the ownership of most of South Uist, and all Eriskay, came into the hands of a Community Company, Stòras Uibhist (www.storasuibhist.com). This is Scotland's biggest community land buyout to date: the 92,000-acre (372.31 km2) estate cost £4.5 million to purchase from the previous owners, a sporting syndicate.

A missile testing range was built in the north west of the island in the 1950s. At the time, there were significant protests: some felt that the local culture would not survive the influx of English speakers! Compton Mackenzie wrote a book about it called Rockets Galore. The range has survived over the decades, testing a succession of weapons and research rockets: the first object to be sent into space from the UK was launched from here in 2015. These days, it is owned by the Ministry of Defence but operated by QinetiQ, the privatised defence research company. Proposals for the range to be run down led to protests over the effect on the local economy, but in 2016 it was announced that it would be operational until at least 2028.

After crossing Eriskay, and the Causeway, the Hebridean Way runs the length of South Uist. Mostly, it follows the main road from south to north, though there are a couple of detours where the minor road system allows. There are views of the higher hills along the way, but the route stays flat and low: there are no big climbs. And whilst the route runs close to the sea at times, to have a proper look at the beaches you will have to make a detour.

The South Uist stretch of the Hebridean Way can be covered quite quickly, but to do so without doing a bit of exploring would be a shame. The west coast is worth a look, and the machair birds and flowers can be truly marvellous. If you have a spare day, a wander over the moor to the east coast or up one of the bigger hills will show you how wild the landscape can be, maybe reveal some interesting archaeology, and probably give sightings of eagles or hen harriers if you keep your eyes open.

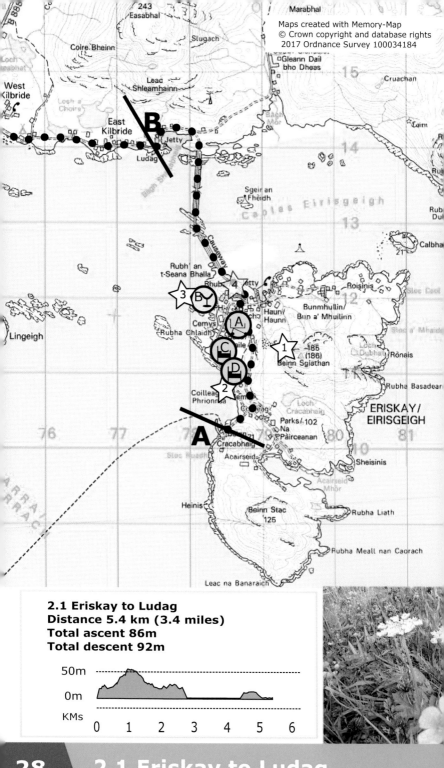

Maps created with Memory-Map
© Crown copyright and database rights
2017 Ordnance Survey 100034184

2.1 Eriskay to Ludag
Distance 5.4 km (3.4 miles)
Total ascent 86m
Total descent 92m

The Route

The ferry arrives on Eriskay at the new harbour, with its curved breakwater. Leaving the slipway, you have no choice but to follow the road left, passing above "Prince Charlie's beach". The road rises steeply, crosses the ridge running down from Ben Scrien, then descends to the village. After the shop, turn right, then take the second left which runs down through a cutting to cross the mile-long causeway to South Uist (opened in 2001). At the north end, follow the road round to the left. Continue past the little bay of Ludag, with its varied collection of boats. At the junction, turn right (left takes you out to the old ferry jetty).

Points of Interest

Eriskay

Sparsely inhabited before the clearances, many evicted families moved to Eriskay in the latter part of the 19th century. A fishing industry developed, leading to a rather different economy and culture to that on the nearby islands more dependent upon crofting. The island is famous for its jumpers: traditionally each one has an individual pattern, knitted by a local woman so that fishermen's bodies can be identified. The small ponies are also famous. Legend has Bruce riding one at Bannockburn.

Prince Charlie's Beach

Charles Edward Stuart landed on the white sand beach by the ferry port on 23rd July 1745, at the start of his ill-fated campaign. A monument behind the dunes commemorates the event. Seeds of the sea bindweed, which grows here, are said to have arrived with him from France on his handkerchief.

Am Politician

The lounge bar is named after the SS Politician which ran aground in the Sound of Eriskay in 1941, inspiring the book and film "Whisky Galore". Some remains can still be seen off Calvay at exceptionally low tides. The ship was carrying 28,000 cases of whisky, banknotes and bicycle parts to Jamaica. Islanders, who had been enduring war time hardships, cared for the crew of the boat, but "salvaged" much of the whisky and some of the banknotes. Customs officials were not amused: the boat was blown up to prevent further raids. Several locals were imprisoned because of their activities after the wreck.

St Michael's Church

Built by islanders in 1903, it incorporates a boat's prow in the altar, an outside handrail for use in strong winds and a bell from the German battleship Derfflinger, scuttled at Scapa Flow in 1919.

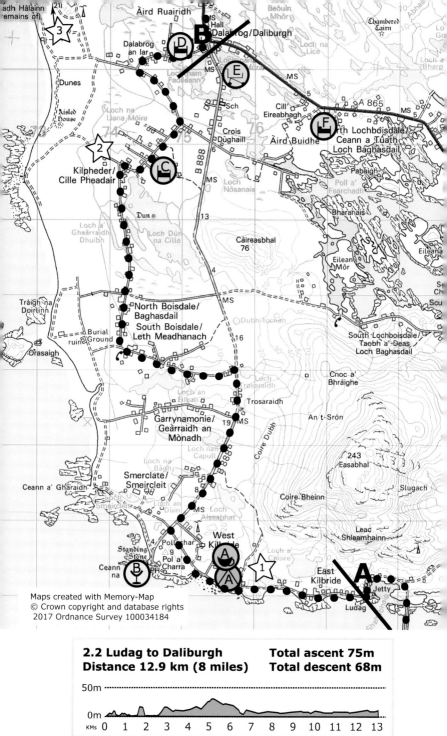

2.2 Ludag to Daliburgh
Distance 12.9 km (8 miles)

Total ascent 75m
Total descent 68m

The Route

Continue along the coast road, passing the walled garden, café and campsite at Kilbride. At the junction, turn right onto the B888 and head north through boggier ground, and a wilder, wetter landscape. Follow the road past a modern Catholic church on a hill, then turn left through South Boisdale and head through the crofting land past lochs. Keep on the main drag until a signed T junction where you turn left, and then take the next right to pass a church. The road will bring you into Daliburgh by a memorial to a local poet, just south of the Borodale Hotel. Turn left and left again to head up the main road.

Points of Interest

Kilbride

St Bride reputedly stepped ashore here, after journeying from Ireland, with an oystercatcher perched on each wrist (the Gaelic name for the bird is Gille-Bhrìde). Kilbride House was here, home of MacDonald of Boisdale, who famously told the newly arrived Bonnie Prince Charlie to go home to France. Later, however, the Prince stayed during his flight. The house is long gone but the walled garden remains: it was the first place where potatoes were cultivated in South Uist in 1742. The Big Garden, as it is called, is open to visitors on occasion and shows what can be grown if the winds are kept at bay (note the frames for the greenhouses!).

Kilpheder

A 2000-year-old wheelhouse was excavated here in the 1950s. Whilst well preserved at the time, it has since deteriorated markedly. A nearby burial cairn (now reconstructed at the Kildonan museum) contained the remains of a woman buried around 700AD. Known as "Kilpheder Kate", her burial is thought to indicate that she was an important person. An incomer, her diet contained very little fish or shellfish.

Hallan

The area in the dunes near the cemetery was inhabited from around 2000BC to 1300AD. Archaeologists have unearthed terraced roundhouses from the Bronze Age: three can be seen by visitors at grid ref NF 731220. Finds include the only prehistoric mummified bodies known from Britain. It is thought that people's daily activities revolved around the house in a clockwise direction, following the sun.

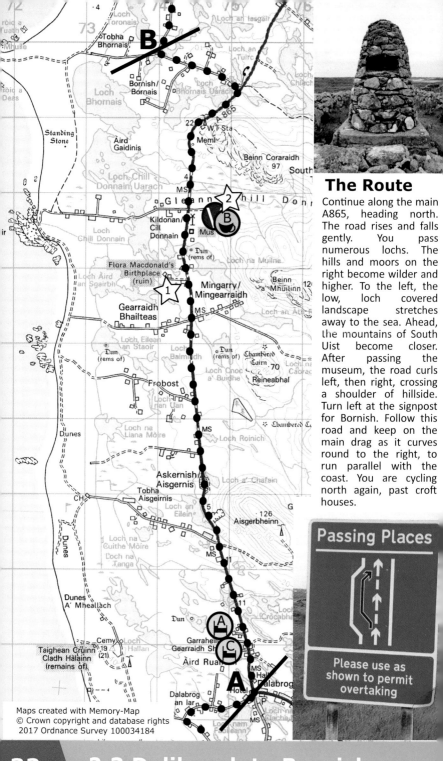

The Route

Continue along the main A865, heading north. The road rises and falls gently. You pass numerous lochs. The hills and moors on the right become wilder and higher. To the left, the low, loch covered landscape stretches away to the sea. Ahead, the mountains of South Uist become closer. After passing the museum, the road curls left, then right, crossing a shoulder of hillside. Turn left at the signpost for Bornish. Follow this road and keep on the main drag as it curves round to the right, to run parallel with the coast. You are cycling north again, past croft houses.

Passing Places

Please use as shown to permit overtaking

Maps created with Memory-Map
© Crown copyright and database rights
2017 Ordnance Survey 100034184

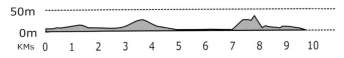

2.3 Daliburgh to Bornish
Distance 9.8 km (6.1 miles)
Total ascent 53m
Total descent 56m

Points of Interest

☆1 Flora Macdonald's birthplace

On the west side of the road, down a small track (signed), a cairn marks the birthplace of Flora Macdonald, the islander famous for helping Charles Edward Stuart escape "over the sea to Skye". However, this was just one incident in her amazing life. Following the Prince's escape to France, she was arrested, taken to London and imprisoned in the Tower. Her story, and courage, led to her being pardoned. She married, and later emigrated to North Carolina where her husband fought for the British in the American Revolutionary War. He was captured by the American rebels and she came back to Britain on a ship that was attacked by privateers. She returned to Skye, where her husband eventually joined her, and she ended her years.

Despite the signs, Flora Macdonald was almost certainly not born in this house, though possibly lived here as a child. The monument was placed here by Clan Donald to commemorate her life. It is a marvellous viewpoint, looking out over the low fields on all sides.

☆2 Kildonan Museum

This fascinating collection of exhibits and recreations of rooms from different houses and buildings, gives a compelling series of pictures of island life, without engaging in misty-eyed nostalgia. It holds a collection of items collected during the 1950s and 60s by a local parish priest, Father John Morrison. The carved Clanranald Stone from the Teampull Mor complex at Howtown is also here. It was stolen, and later recovered from London, in the 1990s. There are also toilets, a café and a shop with local crafts.

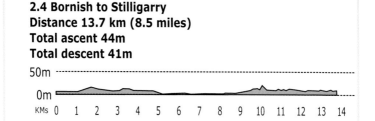

2.4 Bornish to Stilligarry
Distance 13.7 km (8.5 miles)
Total ascent 44m
Total descent 41m

1

Detour to Ardvule

A walk or cycle over rough tracks out to Ardvule takes you past cultivated machair (barley, potatoes etc) to a low peninsular rich in birdlife. Common seals are usually to be seen, hauled out on the rocks. There is a ruined broch (Dun Vulan) and views along the coast to Barra and North Uist. The concrete road (badly damaged in the January 2005 storm) and construction at the end were part of the South Uist missile range.

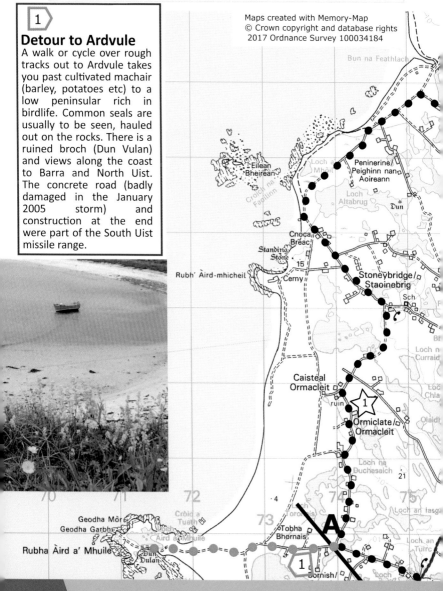

Maps created with Memory-Map
© Crown copyright and database rights
2017 Ordnance Survey 100034184

The Route

Carry on along the minor road through the croftland, passing Ormacleit, and the ruined castle. Keep on the main drag, pass a turn to the right and then go left at a T-junction. The route heads down to the coast, then runs behind a sea wall and along the machair. Follow the road as it curls round to the right and heads back inland past lochs and the township of Tobha Beag (Howbeg), towards the highest hills of South Uist. At the main road turn left and cycle north, climbing gently past the village of Tobha Mor (Howmore) and then descending again. Carry on past Loch Druidibeg, a National Nature Reserve.

Points of Interest

1 Ormacleit Castle

Built in 1701 for MacDonald of Clanranald, it was badly damaged by fire in 1715 (supposedly on the day that MacDonald was killed in battle). The building was abandoned and has never been lived in since.

2 Howbeg

A sign pointing to "The French MacDonald" leads to a memorial at the birthplace of Neil MacEachan (MacDonald) who helped Bonnie Prince Charlie closely over a period of two months in the summer of 1746. He followed the Prince to France, and his son, Jacques, became one of Napoleon's most celebrated marshals. Jacques visited South Uist in 1825, when he was met by large crowds.

3 Howmore

The atmospherically weathered and lichened ruins at Howmore mark the remains of four mediaeval churches and chapels that formed a major centre of learning and religion. In 1990 it was noticed that the carved Clanranald stone, a 350lb block of Carsaig sandstone bearing pictures of a ship and a castle, that usually leant against the chapel walls, had gone missing. The police said no action could be taken, as ownership could not be established! In 1995 the stone turned up at a flat in London. A couple from Canada had found it as they were dealing with the belongings of their recently deceased son. The stone can be seen at the Kildonan museum. There is a Gatliff Trust hostel next to the chapels.

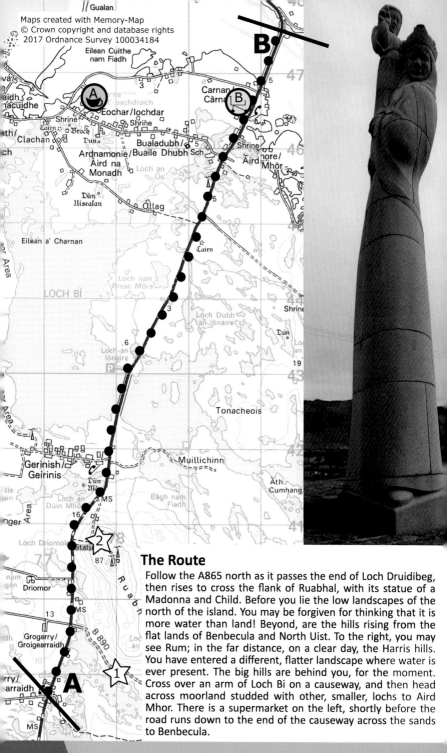

The Route

Follow the A865 north as it passes the end of Loch Druidibeg, then rises to cross the flank of Ruabhal, with its statue of a Madonna and Child. Before you lie the low landscapes of the north of the island. You may be forgiven for thinking that it is more water than land! Beyond, are the hills rising from the flat lands of Benbecula and North Uist. To the right, you may see Rum; in the far distance, on a clear day, the Harris hills. You have entered a different, flatter landscape where water is ever present. The big hills are behind you, for the moment. Cross over an arm of Loch Bi on a causeway, and then head across moorland studded with other, smaller, lochs to Aird Mhor. There is a supermarket on the left, shortly before the road runs down to the end of the causeway across the sands to Benbecula.

2.5 Stilligarry to Causeway
Route distance 9.7 km (6 miles)
Total ascent 26m
Total descent 33m

CAUTION
Otters Crossing

50m
0m
KMs 0 1 2 3 4 5 6 7 8 9 10

Points of Interest

1 Loch Druidibeg

Loch Druidibeg is a National Nature Reserve, encompassing a variety of the habitats to be found on the island. A self-guided nature trail starts from the car park a mile and a half or so down the B890 Loch Skipport road. Loch Skipport itself is a good place to look for birds of prey.

2 Our Lady of the Isles

The 1957 statue by Hew Lorimer looks out from the slopes of Rueval over the loch-studded land and waterscape. Commissioned by Father John Morrison, a local parish priest, it was funded by local people. Nearby is the rocket tracking station known as "Space City".

Section 3 Benbecula,
North Uist and Berneray

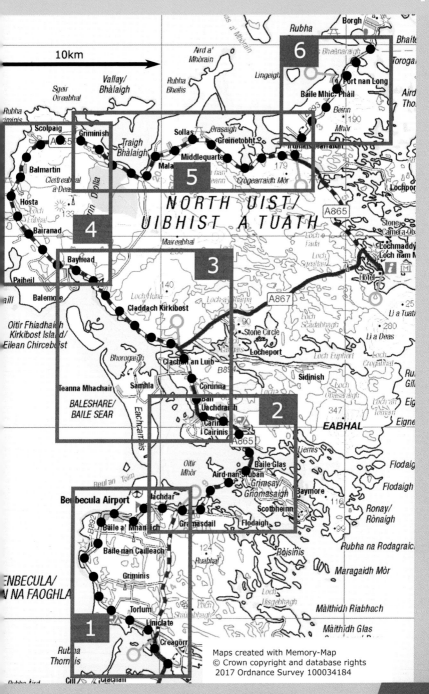

Maps created with Memory-Map
© Crown copyright and database rights
2017 Ordnance Survey 100034184

These three islands each have a different feel, whilst remaining true to the landscape model of the Outer Hebrides: beaches to the west; moorland, hill and lochan to the east. Lower and smaller than South Uist, they all had much larger populations in the past.

Benbecula (in Gaelic Beinn Na Faoghla, mountain of the fords) is low lying, much of it boggy and watery. In Gaelic poetry, it is known as Eilean Dorcha, the Dark Island, the name of a summer music festival. Traditionally owned by the MacDonalds, Benbecula was bought by Gordon of Cluny, and then sold on after the death of Lady Cathcart. It became part of the South Uist Estate, and included in the community buyout in 2006. Balivanich, in the north west of the island, is the main settlement, incorporating the airport, military premises (now run by QinetiQ) and housing unlike anything elsewhere in the Hebrides. The island's population was around 1300 people at the time of the 2011 census.

Benbecula to Berneray

North Uist is an island of contrasts: extensive sands behind a protective chain of islands; flat moorland; low hills and an intricate pattern of fresh and salt water lochs. The population (around 1600 in 2011) inhabits the coast: crofting townships to the west and north, and Lochmaddy, a fine natural harbour, on the east. It has long been a fishing port (four hundred boats operated in the seventeenth century). Traditionally, Lochmaddy has held the courthouse for the southern islands. These days, it also has an arts centre, cafe and museum: Taigh Chearsabaigh.

There are many prehistoric remains on the island. Traditionally, it belonged to the Macruaraidhs, before coming into the hands of the MacDonalds of Sleat. They sold it in 1855 to Sir John Powlett Orde. It has been owned since 1961 by the Granville Family through the North Uist Trust.

Large areas of fertile machair had allowed a relatively large population to develop, though storm damage in the 16th and 18th centuries is known to have been extensive. Extreme events reputedly destroyed dune systems linking to the Monach Isles and Baleshare. Kelp allowed the population to expand further, to around 5000 people in the 1820s. But the collapse of the industry led to emigration, and clearances in the north. Some moved to the east coast, many to Canada. A series of raids took place in the late 19th and early 20th century to try and gain access to the land for those who had been cleared. Today, the population lives mainly by crofting: the moorland is given over to fishing, hunting and peat cutting.

Berneray (from the old Norse for Bjorn's island) is mainly sand and machair. Its causeway link opened officially in 1999. Some years earlier, the island became famous for the Prince of Wales visiting and spending time helping a local crofter. It has a population of around 140.

All three islands are worth exploring as you pass through. Benbecula's highest point, Ruabhal (124m), is easily climbed from the A road for astounding views of a watery world. North Uist's coastline and wildlife will repay the time spent. Berneray's machair is perhaps the finest for summer flowers, and the Gatliff Trust hostel is in a magical spot by the shore.

Maps created with Memory-Map
© Crown copyright and database rights
2017 Ordnance Survey 100034184

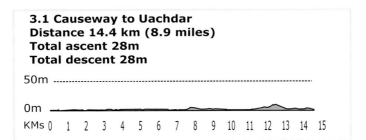

3.1 Causeway to Uachdar
Distance 14.4 km (8.9 miles)
Total ascent 28m
Total descent 28m

The Route

Cycle across the causeway, and follow the A road past the Co-op supermarket on your left and the hotel on your right. At the road junction, turn left onto the B892. This follows the west coast around the island. If you were to carry straight on, the A road across the middle makes for a shorter, but less interesting, journey. The B892 passes Lionacleit (hotel, school and campsite), barely rising and falling. It carries on through low machair farmland, with some large lochs inland. Pass Stinky Bay (you will probably recognise this by the smell!), go through Nunton and into the main settlement of Balivanich. The road runs past modern housing estates and then, heading east, the military base (West Camp) and the old military base (East Camp). It turns left and then right, passing the entrance to the golf course and the airport. The machair stretches away to the north. The road runs down closer to the sea.

Points of Interest

**Borve Castle**

The lichened ruins of Borve Castle are the visible remains of what was once probably the most important castle in the Outer Hebrides. Built in the 14th century, on a small islet in a tidal loch, it was occupied by Clanranald until 1715. Wind-blown sand has filled in the loch and part-covered the ruins: all we see are the two upper floors.

2 Nunton

The graveyard contains the ruins of a mediaeval nunnery, associated with Iona Abbey. Nunton House, now a hostel, is where Flora Macdonald met Bonnie Prince Charlie, disguising him as her maid, Betty Burke, for the journey to Skye. The old steadings opposite are now an art gallery and craft centre. A plaque commemorates the 1923 Nunton Farm land raid.

3 Balivanich

The airport dates from World War II, when the original South Ford Bridge was built to link it to the Lochboisdale steamer port. Post-war, it became the control centre for the Hebrides rocket range.

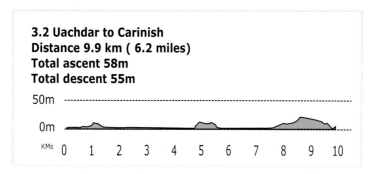

3.2 Uachdar to Carinish
Distance 9.9 km (6.2 miles)
Total ascent 58m
Total descent 55m

The Route

Carry along the B892 to the junction with the A865, then go straight on along the A road (turn left). The road curves to the left and heads out on causeway sections across the sand and rocks towards North Uist. Some of these sections are narrow, others much wider. You may need to give way at times. After crossing the small island of Grimsay, the road curves round again over more small islets to arrive on North Uist proper. It crosses moorland, rises slightly and then comes down into the settlement of Carinish.

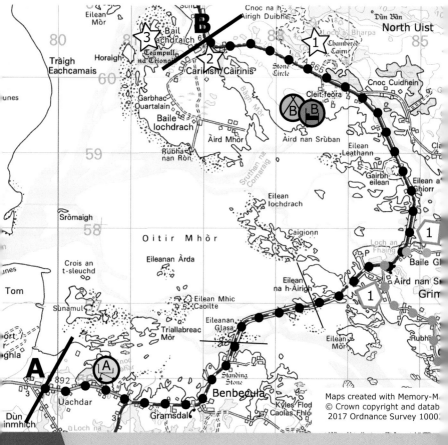

1 > **Detour round Grimsay**
    The Grimsay circuit (9.6km, not shown in full) takes one past Uist Wool's spinning mill and shop, east coast rocky island scenery, and the busy little fishing port at Ceallan, site of the Kallin shellfish shop.

Points of Interest

1 Caravat Bharp

A chambered cairn burial tomb, with stones still piled up to 2m high, can be reached along a path from the car park by a recently planted native woodland. Nearby, later settlements have been uncovered by archaeologists (and peat cutters), suggesting the site must have been important to local people for well over 1500 years.

2 Carinish

A field at the roadside, known as the "Field of Blood", is reputed to be the site of a battle fought in 1601 between the MacDonalds of Sleat and the Macleods of Harris. Following the divorce of a McLeod wife by a MacDonald husband, a group of 60 McLeods marched here intent on revenge. They were met by 16 MacDonalds who attacked them fiercely and, despite their smaller numbers, emerged victorious.

3 Trinity Temple

The ruins of Teampull na Trionad, a mediaeval church, are believed to represent one of the most important sites of mediaeval learning in the Outer Hebrides. Originally a 12th-13th century monastery, it is thought that the building was extended in the 14th century, before being destroyed during the reformation. The buildings have been restored somewhat, but the ruins are atmospheric and the nearby mounds evocative: what secrets lie under them, what stories of past lives do they hold?

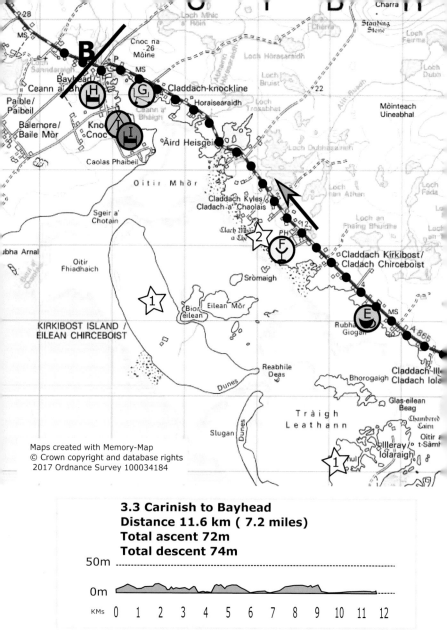

3.3 Carinish to Bayhead
Distance 11.6 km (7.2 miles)
Total ascent 72m
Total descent 74m

The Route

Carry on along the A865. At the junction with the A867 (to Lochmaddy) carry straight on. The road rises past the smokehouse, then gently undulates. To the right, lochan studded moorland rises gently towards the hills. To the left, the ground falls to the sea, sandy beaches and a line of machair islands. Continue along past the croft houses and pub at Cladach Kirkibost, and the turn to the right known as the Committee Road. Run gently down to Ceann a Bhaigh and the Bayhead Stores

Detour to Barpa Langass

Turning right on the A867 will bring you in a couple of miles to the impressive Barpa Langass chambered cairn on the side of Beinn Langais. At the bottom of the small road before the cairn, just beyond the Langass Lodge Hotel, the Pobull Fhinn stone circle stands on a ledge dug out by prehistoric people. The RSPB run otter walks from the hotel in summer.

Points of Interest

1 Baleshare and Kirkibost

Offshore, the long, low islands of Baleshare (population about 50) and Kirkibost (now uninhabited) catch the eye. Cut off at high tide, Baleshare was linked by Causeway in 1962. The name means "east town": was there a "west town" washed away by the legendary storm that cut off the Monach Isles in the 16th or 17th century? Baleshare is so flat that it does not boast a single contour line on the Ordnance Survey map.

2 The Committee Road

Built in the 1840s to provide famine relief work, the Committee Road cuts across the island to Sollas on the north coast. Men working on the road were paid a penny-halfpenny's worth of meal a day, their wives a pennyworth. The road runs past peat cuttings, and can offer good views of birds of prey (short-eared owls, hen harrier and merlin) on the moorland.

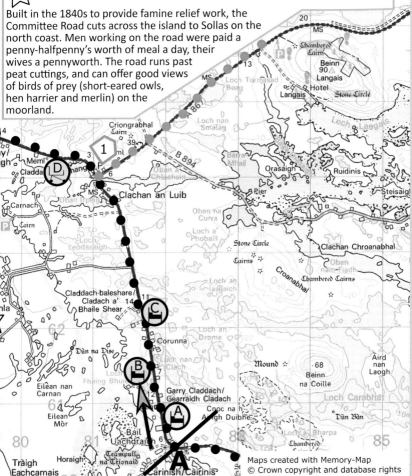

Maps created with Memory-Map
© Crown copyright and database rights
2017 Ordnance Survey 100034184

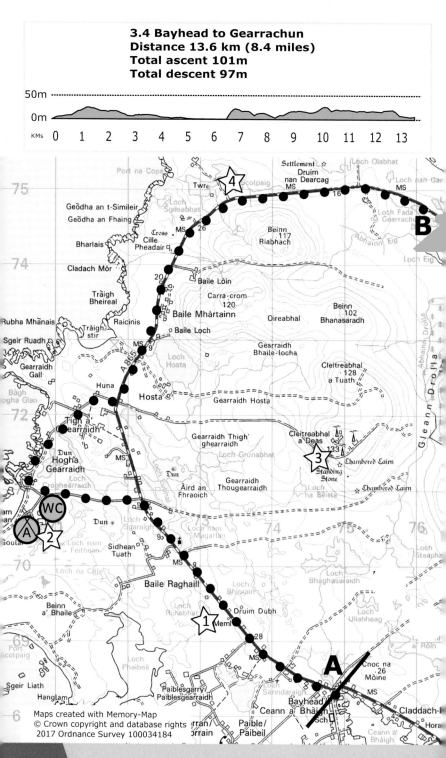

3.4 Bayhead to Gearrachun
Distance 13.6 km (8.4 miles)
Total ascent 101m
Total descent 97m

The Route

Head gradually uphill to the land raid memorial, then descend to the church at Balranald. Continue along the A road, before turning left towards the RSPB reserve at the signs. The road runs through machair, and at the junction follow the narrow road to the right (carry straight on for the reserve). Cross the croftland to come back to the A road. Turn left and follow it through rich machair past the show ground. The road climbs and the fertile machair soils give way to moorland as you turn east. The view over Loch Scolpaig to the cliffs of Rubha Ghriminis is impressive. Carry on through the moorland: the South Harris hills and the fabulous beach scenery of Traigh Bhalaigh come into view.

Points of Interest

1 Paiblesgarry Land Raid Memorial

Balranald estate was raided in 1921, after encouragement from the local MP, Dr Murray of Lewis. The raiders, sentenced to 60 days in prison, were welcomed home with bonfires. Shortly afterwards, land was allocated at Balranald, Paiblesgarry, Tigharry and Hogharry.

2 Balranald Bird Reserve

The Royal Society for the Protection of Birds has managed the reserve since 1966. It contains a variety of machair, croftland, rocky coastal and sandy beach habitats, and has good numbers of breeding waders, corn buntings (their song sounds like a bunch of rattling keys) and corncrake (whose song sounds like a piece of paper rubbing along a comb). The summer flowers can be spectacular, including large numbers of corn marigolds. Access is free at all times: there is a self-guided trail around the reserve and displays in an old croft house. The adjacent campsite sells refreshments.

3 Cleitrabhal

A series of prehistoric sites on the hill include a 30m long, five chambered cairn, a wheelhouse built into the cairn and standing stone. The hillside offers fine views out to sea (to the Monach Isles and St Kilda on a clear day) and across the moorland. It is the site of a missile tracking station linked to the South Uist range.

4 Loch Scolpaig

The tower on Loch Scolpaig is, apparently, one of Scotland's most photographed views. The castellated folly was built in the 1830s as a famine relief project by Dr Macleod, the island's factor. When the water level is low it can be accessed by stepping stones.

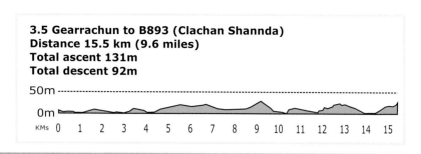

3.5 Gearrachun to B893 (Clachan Shannda)
Distance 15.5 km (9.6 miles)
Total ascent 131m
Total descent 92m

The Route

Continue on the A road around the shores of Traigh Bhalaigh. The forestry on the right comes to an end, and the north end of the Committee Road is passed. There are picturesque houses with stupendous views of the beach. Head through the crofting townships of Malacleit, Solas and Greinetobht. The road rises and falls gently, curls round in front of a beach, then rises and falls again to the sea. The beach views are fantastic. Climb inland towards forestry and a quarry. At the junction with the B893 turn left and proceed along past modern houses and older ruins. Turn offs to the left lead down to the beaches and machair.

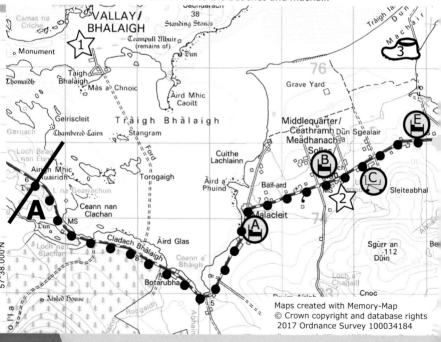

Maps created with Memory-Map
© Crown copyright and database rights
2017 Ordnance Survey 100034184

Points of Interest

 Vallay

Vallay island, accessed by a causeway across the tidal sands, has been uninhabited since 1945 when the then owner, George Beveridge, was killed in a boating accident. The ruined mansion was the family home. A 1960s scheme to reclaim some of the bay and grow flower bulbs came to nothing.

 Sollas

Scene of a conflict when Lord Macdonald evicted over 600 people in 1849. There is a monument to the resettling of the croftland in 1899.

3 Udal Machair Walk

From the turning in Greinetobht out along the Udal peninsular: sea and sand meet, under a magic, open sky. Follow the shoreline out to the cemetery of the Macleans of Boreray, climb a huge sand-dune hill for fabulous views, and return via untrodden coves and ancient sites. The wheelhouses, "jelly baby houses", Viking settlements and Neolithic sites are recognised as some of the most important in the Hebrides. Along the way, you'll barely see a soul, but may well chance upon short-eared owls, eagles and otters, together with a fabulous flora in summer. A walk leaflet can be found on the Visit Outer Hebrides website- www.visitouterhebrides.co.uk

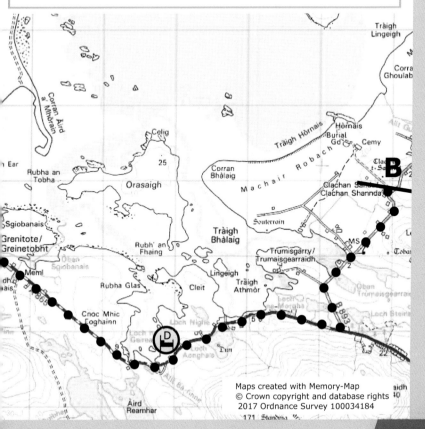

Maps created with Memory-Map
© Crown copyright and database rights
2017 Ordnance Survey 100034184

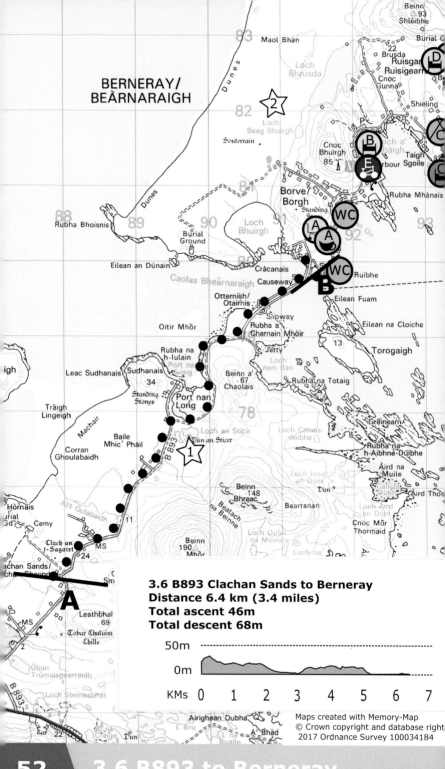

3.6 B893 Clachan Sands to Berneray
Distance 6.4 km (3.4 miles)
Total ascent 46m
Total descent 68m

The Route

Continue along the road and turn right by a loch just before Port nan Long. Follow the minor road round to the next junction. Turn left to the causeway. Cross it. The ferry to Harris (four crossings a day in summer) leaves from the slipway at the far end, though is often moored at the near end! The terminal has toilets, waiting room and Wi-Fi. Carry on to see the village, beaches and machair of Berneray. The ferry weaves its way through the low islands of the Sound of Harris. Can you see the sea eagles on the islets?

Points of Interest

An Sticir

The small tidal loch of An Sticir contains the ruins of a late mediaeval hall built in a 2000-year-old broch on an island reached by a causeway from another island, in turn reached by its own causeway. There are similarities to the site at Finlaggan on Islay, where the Lords of the Isles had their council. In 1601, Hugh MacDonald was seized here by his enemies, before being taken away to a horrible death on Skye.

Berneray

The small island of Berneray consists mainly of beach and machair: it boasts magnificent flowers in summer. It is rabbit-free (note the causeway's cattle grids and wired gates). The Old Nurse's Cottage is a museum of human and natural history, and there is a Gatliff Trust hostel beyond the village, overlooking the Sound of Harris. The Giant Macaskill (Aonghas Mor MacAsgaill) was born on Berneray before his family emigrated to Nova Scotia around 1831. At the height of 7ft 9inches (2.36m) he was said to be the world's tallest man and capable of prodigious feats of strength. A memorial at the southern end of the island commemorates his life. The remains of a Pictish square burial cairn can be seen by the ferry.

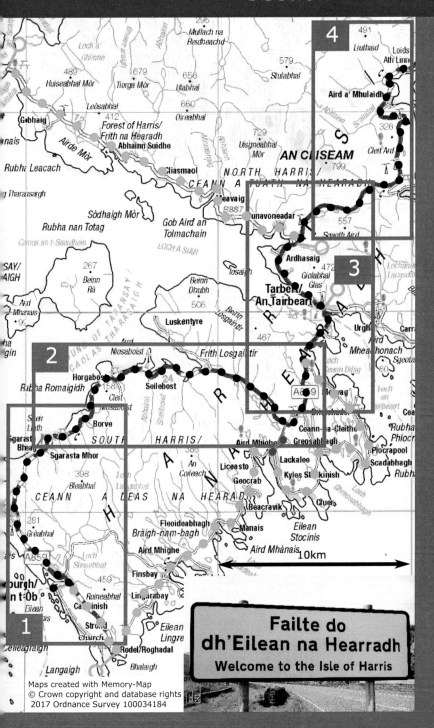

Failte do
dh'Eilean na Hearradh
Welcome to the Isle of Harris

Harris is the southernmost third of the biggest island in the Outer Hebrides. Its Gaelic name, Hearadh meaning "heights", contrasts it with lower-lying Lewis to the North. To be honest, though, the dividing line between the two is a historical contrivance. It is said the division occurred when the land was split between the sons of Leod (progenitor to the MacLeods). For centuries, they were separate: up until 1974 they were part of different local government areas (Lewis being part of Ross and Cromarty, and Harris Inverness). Now they are both part of Comhairle nan Eilean, the former Western Isles Council, but have a different feel. Harris is much less densely populated, and wilder. It has relatively few people: 1,916 in 2011. About a third live in the village of Tarbert, which lies on a narrow isthmus separating more mountainous North Harris from the lower south. South Harris can itself be divided into two parts: the west coast beaches of gold or white shell sand, and the inland and east coast rock, moorland, water and bog.

During the 1790s, when the island was still owned by the MacLeods, people were encouraged to settle on the east coast as part of a fishery development scheme. In 1834, George Murray, 5th Earl of Dunmore, bought Harris for £60,000. Clearances followed: the people of South Harris were ejected from their homes by armed soldiers and a posse of Glasgow policemen. The island passed from father to son to grandson. Amhuinnsuidhe Castle was built by the 7th Earl in 1864 as a hunting lodge. His wife was responsible for the development of the Harris Tweed industry. In 1919, Lord Leverhulme bought the island, and announced his ambitious development plans. But it came to naught, and the island was sold off in lots on his death. More recently, the North Harris Estate was bought in 2003 by the North Harris Trust. They aim to develop it for the benefit of the residents: wildlife tourism and renewable energy are part of the plan. Similarly, the West Harris Trust bought their land from the Scottish Government in 2010.

Arriving by ferry at Leverburgh, one is faced with a decision: which of two great bicycle routes will you take? The Hebridean Way follows the main road along the west coast past some of the finest beaches and sand scenery in Britain: it glows even when the mist is down and the rain is lashing. The route then cuts inland and crosses a rocky pass to Tarbert, with its shops, hotels and new distillery. On the other hand, the "Golden Road" up the east coast, so-called after the amount it cost to build, is also a joy. It passes the mediaeval church at Rodel, with its sculptures and tombs, before heading through a landscape of bare stone, heather, small coves, lochans and crofting townships. It's a joy to ride: a constant series of exhilarating short descents and small climbs, twisting and turning through an ever-changing landscape that almost defies description, but always inspires wonder: how did people live here? How do people live here? For this is where the majority of the population of South Harris live: in the 18th and 19th century people were cleared from the fertile machair of the west to make way for sheep farms. Somehow, they made a living amongst the rocks and bog by the sea.

Perhaps the best thing is to do both routes. Take an extra day and cycle the "South Harris ring", stopping at the art galleries and cafes along the way, and having some time on the beaches. It makes for a very good day. You won't be the first to add to your journey time in this way. Another great bike ride is out west towards Hushinish: lots of ups and downs but impressive mountain and coastal scenery, including the strangeness of Amhuinnsuidhe Castle. Rhenigidale makes for an energetic detour, and there are dozens of great walks too.

After Tarbert, the Hebridean Way goes into the mountains and rises to its highest point beneath An Cliseam, highest hill in the Western Isles. A proper mountain pass is crossed, followed by a sweeping descent to the Lewis border on the shores of Loch Seaforth, a twisted, contorted sea loch penetrating to the heart of the land. Along the way you may well see eagles: Harris boasts one of the highest densities of golden eagle territories anywhere in Europe. There are sea eagles too, not to mention the otters and seals.

Harris 57

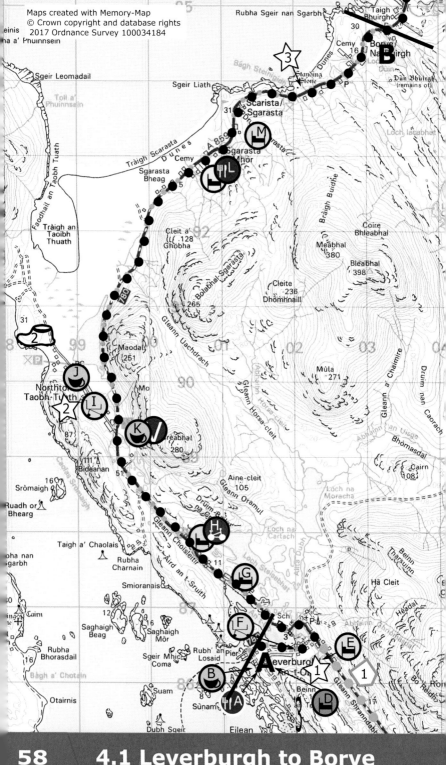

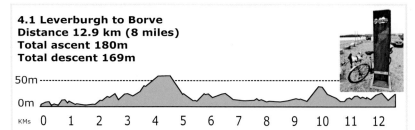

4.1 Leverburgh to Borve
Distance 12.9 km (8 miles)
Total ascent 180m
Total descent 169m

The Route
Turn left after leaving the ferry at Leverburgh, and then right, following the short one-way system. Follow this minor road to the junction with the A859 and turn left. You will follow this road for the next 48 miles! After leaving the village, head up a shallow glen, with low woodland to the left. At the watershed, the fabulous beaches of West Harris are revealed. Descend to the planned township of Northton, pass the loch and head north between the dunes and the grassy fields. There are occasional climbs and descents, and views out to Taransay and the ocean. In the distance lie the North Harris hills.

Detours and walks

1 Cycle Detour- Rodel and the Golden Road
Even if you are not cycling the Golden Road, it is worth visiting the restored mediaeval church of St Clement at Rodel. There are outside carvings of a Sheila-na-gig and male equivalent, and elaborate tombs inside. Legend says that the Countess of Dunmore ordered her ghillie to fire his gun at the carvings because of their indecent nature. The hotel, built as a mansion for the Laird of Harris, is also worth a look.

2 Walk-Toe Head
Toe Head offers sea stacks, arches, seabirds and marine mammals. On the headland to the south lie the remains of a small, late mediaeval chapel with footings of an Iron Age broch and prehistoric settlement mound nearby.

Points of Interest

1 Leverburgh
Lord Leverhulme planned to transform the small settlement of An-T-Ob into a major fishing port of 10,000 people. He began works to remove rocks in the harbour and install deep-sea fishing infrastructure. After his death, the £250,000 installations were sold for £5000 to a demolition company.

2 Northton
A crofting township developed after World War 1 by the Board of Agriculture. The Seallam! Centre has exhibitions on local history and landscape, and a genealogical resource. A centre built to commemorate local lad William MacGillivray, one of Scotland's finest natural historians, has closed, but the building houses the Temple Café overlooking the loch. Nearby is some very impressive machair and salt marsh.

3 Scarasta-Clach Steinagaidh
A standing stone on the coast looking out towards the island of Taransay. When erected, 4,500 or so years ago, it was part of a circle: some other fallen stones can be seen.

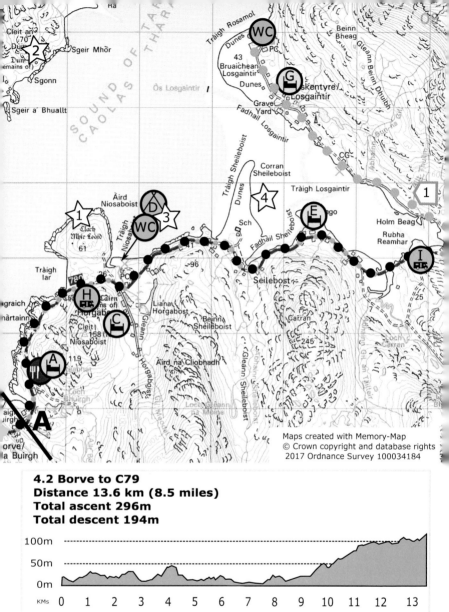

4.2 Borve to C79
Distance 13.6 km (8.5 miles)
Total ascent 296m
Total descent 194m

The Route

The A859 flanks the coast, cuts across headlands. The hillsides get rockier and wilder, the beaches and dunes more dramatic. Striking new buildings, such as the West Harris Trust's Talla na Mara, make the most of views out to sea, to Taransay and to the Harris Hills. Beyond Seilebost, where a silvery spit stretches across the estuary, the road heads inland. It passes saltmarsh, crosses a causeway, then rises slowly and steadily to a 500m hill pass. The upgraded surface is smooth. You may see greenshank and divers on the lochans. Note the tarmacked peat cutting turnoffs. The C79 turn near the top leads towards Lickisto, Stockinish and the Golden Road.

Detours

  Luskentyre

A three mile ride from the main road along the estuary. The Luskentyre Harris Tweed Company at No 6 have supplied Nike and Clarks shoes with fabric. The cemetery served people from the east coast, where the ground is unsuitable for burials. Norman MacCaig's poem "By the Graveyard, Luskentyre" celebrates those who know the land and seascapes.

Points of Interest

At the end of the Nisabost peninsular, Clach Mhic-Leoid is a 3m high standing stone looking across to Taransay and another, matching, stone. It has been claimed that there are alignments with equinoctial sunsets behind the St Kildan island of Boreray.

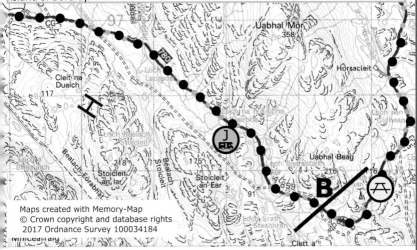

Maps created with Memory-Map
© Crown copyright and database rights
2017 Ordnance Survey 100034184

  Taransay

Offshore, lies the island of Taransay. Uninhabited since 1974, it was used in 2000 for the TV series "Castaway" that brought Ben Fogle to fame. Since then, it has been sold, and is used as holiday accommodation and for grazing. The Sound of Taransay is important for seabirds, particularly in winter. You may also see seals and otters.

  Horgabost

Dunes and machair next to a fine beach, with a campsite and toilets.

  Seilebost

A breath-taking white sandy beach, with a spit stretching across the estuary. The West Harris Trust, who acquired the local land from the Scottish Office in 2010, have motorhome and caravan hook ups at the old school.

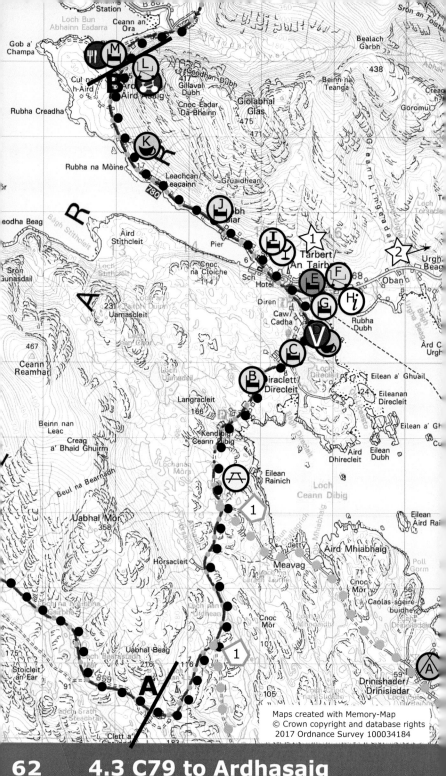

4.3 C79 to Ardhasaig
Distance 11.2 km (7 miles)
Total ascent 201m
Total descent 278m

The Route

Climb the final heights to the pass, then descend through a rocky, lochan-studded landscape. A picnic site offers views, on a fine day, to the islands of Scalpay and the Shiants. Following clearance of black rats from the latter, in 2017 storm petrels were heard calling for the first time.

Descend towards Tarbert: take care on the descent. The roads around the village can be surprisingly busy, particularly at ferry times. The Hebridean Way carries straight on past the village and out along the north shore of West Loch Tarbert. After the ups and downs there is a mile or so of flat cycling above the sea, before a slight rise and then descent brings you to the small hamlet of Ardhasaig.

Detours

1 The Golden Road

Roads off to the rocky "moonscape" of the east coast of the island are passed on the way down to Tarbert.

Points of Interest

1 Tarbert

The village is very much the capital of Harris: around a third of the island's population live here. Ferries link with Uig on Skye. There are shops (including the treasure trove emporium of Akram's general store), a Tourist Information Centre, hotels, hostel and cafes. The Harris Distillery opened in 2015, with café and tours. There is now a one-way system. Despite the product's name, little tweed is made in Harris, though there is a shop opposite the distillery. The Gaelic word "Tarbert" mean low isthmus: the East and West Lochs are separated by only a few hundred metres of low ground. Projected sea level rises in the face of global climate change may lead to difficulties. The village also houses the offices of the North Harris Trust, who bought much of the island as a community buyout in 2003.

2 Scalpay

An island in East Loch Tarbert (not on this map) with good natural harbours and famous for its fishing fleet. The bridge to the tight-knit community opened in 1998.

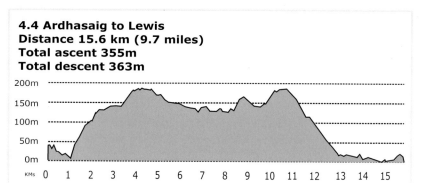

4.4 Ardhasaig to Lewis
Distance 15.6 km (9.7 miles)
Total ascent 355m
Total descent 363m

The Route

The A859 climbs steeply to the 189m (620ft) pass between Clisham (799m/ 2621ft, to the north) and Sgaoth Aird (559m/ 1833ft). This is true mountain country, with dramatic views on a clear day. The road falls slightly, before contouring with fine views of the Loch Seaforth fjord cutting to the heart of the island. After another, more gentle, ascent to 187m (a small wooden bridge marks the top if the weather is cloudy), the road descends through boulder fields in steep sweeping curves. Quickly, you will cross the Vigadale River into Lewis.

Difficulties

The first part of the ascent is steepest: the gradient lessens after the first quarry turn. The yellow posts by the road side are snow poles: be aware of the weather! Take care on the descents: keep your eyes on the road!

Detours

Cycle Detour to Hushinish 1

A 13 mile (each way) ride along the shore of West Loch Tarbert at the foot of the Harris hills. Cycle through dramatic scenery, walk up to the Glen Meavaig golden eagle observatory (golden eagle sightings are not guaranteed, but the dramatic scenery is), pass by a magnificent Victorian castle and end up on a wild coast at a fantastic beach.

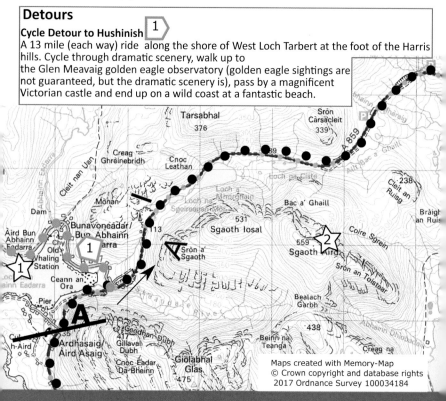

Maps created with Memory-Map
© Crown copyright and database rights
2017 Ordnance Survey 100034184

Detours 2

2

Rhenigidale
Five miles each way (steep up and down) to a remote community and Gatliff Trust hostel. Electricity arrived in 1980, the road in 1990.

Points of Interest

1 Buonavoneader

Just across the water from Ardhasaig, a tall brick chimney marks the remains of a whaling station originally built by Norwegians in 1904. A Leverhulme project, it ran until the 1930s.

2 North Harris Hills

The wild landscape of rocks, bog, lochans and mountains is a big part of the Harris tourist draw. There are marvellous opportunities for wildlife watching: it has one of the densest populations of golden eagles in Europe (around 13 territories). The North Harris Trust run a Mountain Festival each year and have built a wind energy scheme on the hills.

3 Clisham

An Cliseam: 779m (not on map)
The highest hill in the Outer Hebrides qualifies as a "Corbett". Ascents are usually made from the roadside carparks at the pass and are straightforward. The views are stunning on a clear day.

4 Scaladale Centre

Run by Lewis and Harris Youth Clubs, this is an outdoor activity centre. It also offers hostel accommodation.

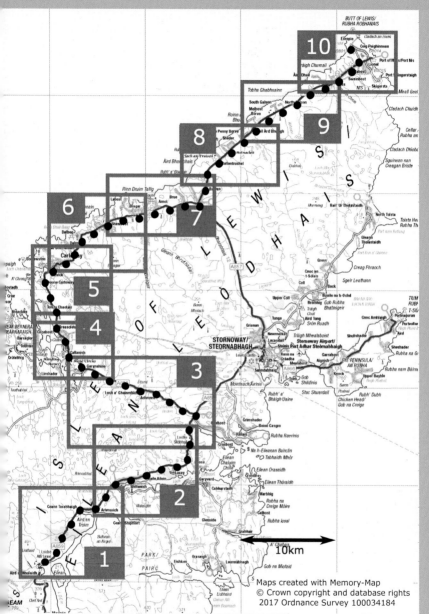

Lewis is big, Lewis is different. You will soon know you have arrived somewhere else. It is far larger, and has fewer beaches than the other islands. It has two thirds of the Outer Hebrides' population; almost half of these live in a town! Stornoway draws commuters and shoppers from all over. As a result, Lewis seems less remote than the other islands. But there is still a feeling of being on the edge and close to the wild. People live round the coast. Inland lie huge, brown moors: the name Lewis comes from a Gaelic word (Leodhas) meaning marshy.

Traditionally, Lewis was owned by the Macleods, though following the failed invasions by the Fife Adventurers in the early 17th century, James VI of Scotland (1st of England) gave it to the Mackenzies. In 1844, they sold the island to James Matheson. Co-founder of the Jardine Matheson trading empire, he had made his fortune selling opium to the Chinese. He built Lews Castle in Stornoway as his residence. The building, whose wooded grounds are unlike anything else in the Outer Hebrides, has recently reopened as the Museum nan Eilean.

In 1918, Lord Leverhulme bought the island, planning to turn it into a fishing hub. But the crofters wanted land, and opposed his plans. Rejected, he offered the island to its residents. Only Stornoway took up the offer. He sold the rest to various parties.

Stornoway, one of the most sheltered natural ports in north west Scotland, has long been an important fishing harbour. More recently, it has seen oil rig manufacturing, and latterly, wind turbines. It is the service and administrative centre for the islands, and seat of Comhairle nan Eilean Siar, previously the Western Isles Council. It is not a beautiful town, though it is worth exploring the grounds of Lews Castle, taking in the museum (including the Lewis chessmen) and visiting the An Lanntair arts centre.

The Hebridean Way travels up the A859 by Loch Seaforth. After crossing a couple of low passes, it heads west across the sparsely populated moorland. Reaching the west coast, it heads north through a series of crofting townships a short distance inland from the sea. Finally, you reach the north point, the Butt of Lewis. Along the way, you pass a wealth of historical sites and interest. The Lewis landscape may not be as scenically beautiful as the islands further south, but the evidence of the human history is arguably far more interesting.

Lewis offers much more than just the route of the Hebridean Way. A journey out to the Pairc peninsular in the south east takes you to an indented, tortuous landscape where people have made a living for centuries. Many were evicted in Victorian times to make way for sporting (i.e. deer stalking) interests: this is a prime place to see eagles.

The road to the West (Uig) leads to mountains and glacial scenery, fantastic beaches and isolated crofting communities. The Lewis chessmen, iconic Viking walrus tusk pieces, were found here in the 19th century. Roads across the centre of the island bring the cyclist into contact with the immensity of the peat bog: there are good chances of seeing hen harriers quartering the moor. Journeys up the east coast beyond Stornoway, to Tolsta and the "Bridge to Nowhere", lead to symbols of opposition to Lord Leverhulme. The Point peninsular boasts rock that is, for once, not Lewisian gneiss.

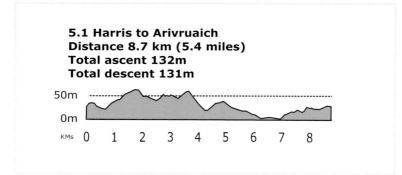

5.1 Harris to Arivruaich
Distance 8.7 km (5.4 miles)
Total ascent 132m
Total descent 131m

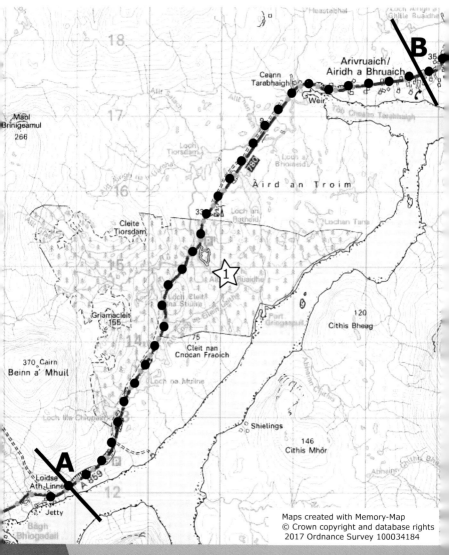

The Route

Follow the A859 above the shores of Loch Seaforth, with the big hill slopes above you on the left. Climb to pass over a spur, and head through the Aline Community Woodlands, a plantation that shows trees can be grown in the Outer Hebrides on a large scale. Head across moorland and descend to the head of Loch Seaforth.

Aline Community Woodland

Covering an area of over 600 hectares, this was bought by The Erisort Trust in 2007. They have set up several commercial activities, and native trees are being planted to replace the exotic Sitka spruce and lodgepole pine that have suffered from pine beauty moth. There are a number of trails in the woodland, including one down to the shore of Loch Seaforth. It is a stop on the Bird of Prey Trail: golden eagles from the hills are regularly seen, as well as white tailed eagles by the sea. Sparrowhawks and buzzards live in the woodlands.

5.2 Arivruaich to Shobhail
Distance 15.2 km (9.4 miles)
Total ascent 247m
Total descent 240m

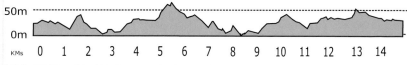

The Route

Continue along the A859, crossing the neck between Lochs Seaforth and Erisort. Pass turnoffs to Eishken and the Pairc peninsular, then climb through the village of Balallan. Descend to the River Laxay, pass through the village, then turn north, across an undulating moorland with many lochs. At the Keose junction, you pass the first "four quartered" Lewis bus shelter.

⟨1⟩ Charles Edward Stuart Monument

The Prince landed here, just 18 days after the defeat at Culloden, whilst heading from Scalpay to Arnish near Stornoway.

⟨2⟩ Pairc Raiders Monument

In November 1887, local people raided Pairc after Lady Matheson turned it over to deer forest. The sporting tenant and Secretary of State panicked, sending in the Royal Navy and soldiers. Six of the leaders were arrested and tried in Edinburgh. All were acquitted. The 1994 monument contains stones from the homes of the arrested men, as well as other symbolic items.

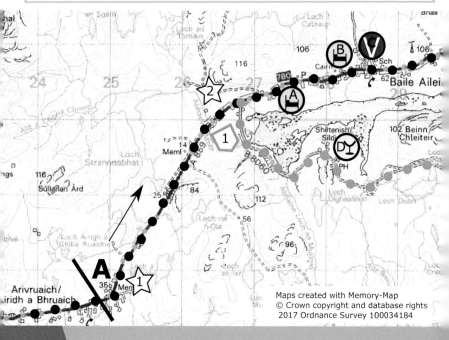

Maps created with Memory-Map
© Crown copyright and database rights
2017 Ordnance Survey 100034184

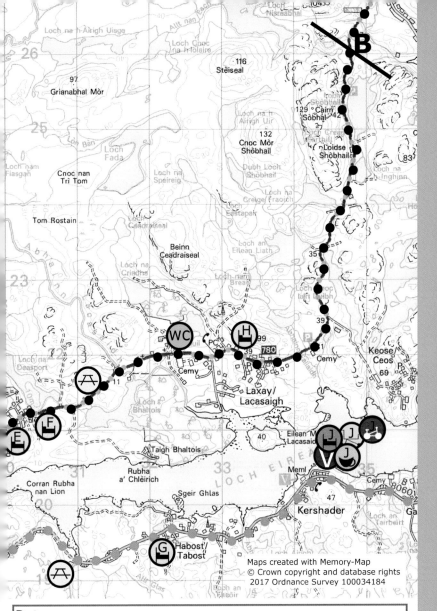

Detour

1 Pairc

The rugged Pairc peninsular is still mostly a shooting and fishing estate. Part was recently the subject of a successful community buyout, though this was opposed by the previous landowner. The rugged area is home to at least 6 pairs of sea eagles. There are small crofting communities along the north and east coasts. The Ravenspoint Community Centre at Kershader runs a shop, exhibition, hostel and café, and can do bike hire. It is also a stop on the Bird of Prey Trail. They are keen to promote the "Ring of Pairc" as a challenging bike ride.

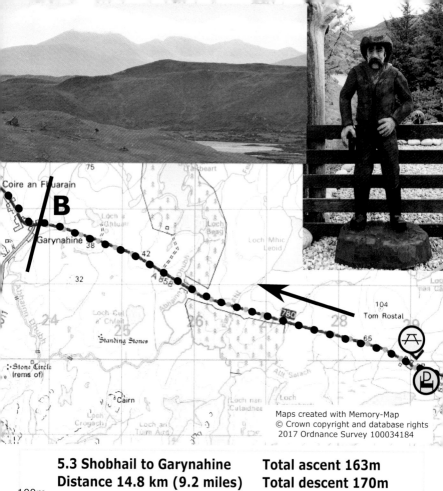

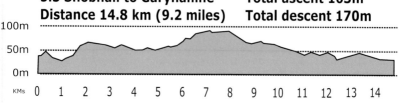

5.3 Shobhail to Garynahine
Distance 14.8 km (9.2 miles)
Total ascent 163m
Total descent 170m

Maps created with Memory-Map
© Crown copyright and database rights
2017 Ordnance Survey 100034184

The Route

The road passes Soval Lodge on the left, then descends before rising again slowly. Pass the minor road to Leurbost then turn left onto the A858 at the main junction. Head west, over the moor, ascending gradually to Achmore, the only village in Lewis that is not close to the sea. There is a real feeling of exposure here; of being in a big, open landscape with views south over the loch-filled moorland to the hills of Harris and south Lewis. Gradually, the road falls towards the coast, crossing the flanks of hills to the north. Plantations show that trees can grow, even in this exposed spot. At the small hamlet of Garynahine, the road to Uig and Great Bernera goes off to the left.

Difficulties

None, though the route crosses exposed moorland roads, open to the weather. The A858 is the main road to the west coast, so can be busy with fast traffic.

Detours

 To Stornoway

Either via the main A859 or the quieter moorland road from Achmore, which passes shielings and lochs and peat cuttings. There are good opportunities to see hen harriers quartering the moor from this road.

Points of Interest

 Achmore Stone Circle

For many years, local crofters had said that there was a stone circle being exposed by peat cutting on the moor above the township. This was confirmed in 1981 by local archaeologists. Around 20 stones have been found, mostly fallen. The site remains in a peat cutting area, though has now been signposted from the road.

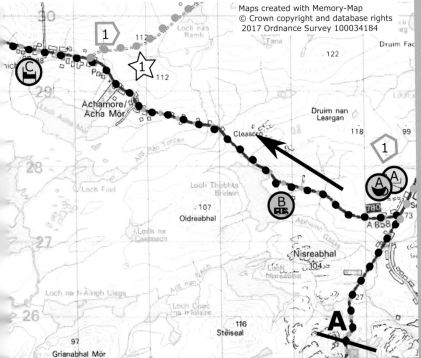

Maps created with Memory-Map
© Crown copyright and database rights
2017 Ordnance Survey 100034184

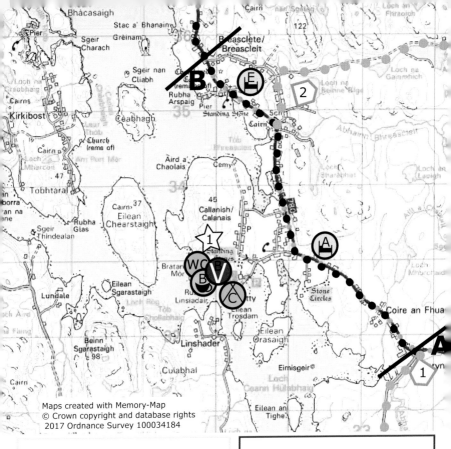

5.4 Garynahine to Breasclete
Distance 5.3 km (3.3 miles)
Total ascent 57m
Total descent 59m

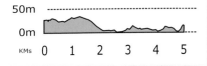

Route
The Hebridean way continues along the A858, heading north along the coast. The sea, off to the left, appears to be entirely surrounded by surprisingly low land. You will almost certainly want to turn left to see the Callanish stone circle, but the route carries along the road to Breasclete.

Difficulties
None really, though the road can be busy with tourist traffic and coaches.

Detours

1 Uig and Great Bernera

Turn left at Garynahine on the B8011. This takes you across the moor to the island of Great Bernera (beaches, lochs and a small community surviving thanks to a bridge) or the west coast area of Uig (fantastic beaches and isolated communities).

2 Pentland Road

Turn right in Breasclete for the Pentland Road towards Stornoway. This is a quiet, single tracked road with passing places that cuts across the middle of the great moor past shielings and peat cuttings. It boasts a feeling of low, wild remoteness.

Points of Interest

 1 Callanish

The complexes of standing stones at Callanish are perhaps second only to Stonehenge in terms of their archaeological importance.

Erected between 4,500 and 5,000 years ago, the main site consists of circles and lines of stones making up a "Celtic Cross" shape. There is a tomb near the central circle and a massive, 4.8m high, central monolith. At least three other stone circles are nearby (Callanish ll, lll,and IV). The area was obviously one of great importance, though what that importance was remains a mystery. A striking feature of the site is its open setting, with wide views over the land and seascape towards the distant hills. Various "alignments" between the moon and visible landscape features such as Clisham have been proposed, but none are totally convincing.

Understandably, there are legends concerning heathen worship and enchanted figures becoming petrified. The stones have long been known: perhaps this is the winged temple described by the ancient Greek writer Herodotus. The Greek historian Diodorus Siculus (55 BC) wrote that there was an island called Hyperborea (meaning "Far to the North") where a round temple stood from which the moon appeared only a little distance above the earth every 19 years. Martin Martin, in the late 17th century, was told "it was a place appointed for worship in the time of heathenism , and that the chief druid or priest stood near the big stone in the centre, from whence he addressed himself to the people that surrounded him". In the mid-19th century, the accumulated peat was removed, revealing the stones' true stature: atmospheric and impressive, they are of Lewisian gneiss and display bands of different colours.

There is a visitor centre with a café and "Story of the Stones" exhibition. Entry to the stones themselves is free at any time.

http://www.callanishvisitorcentre.co.uk

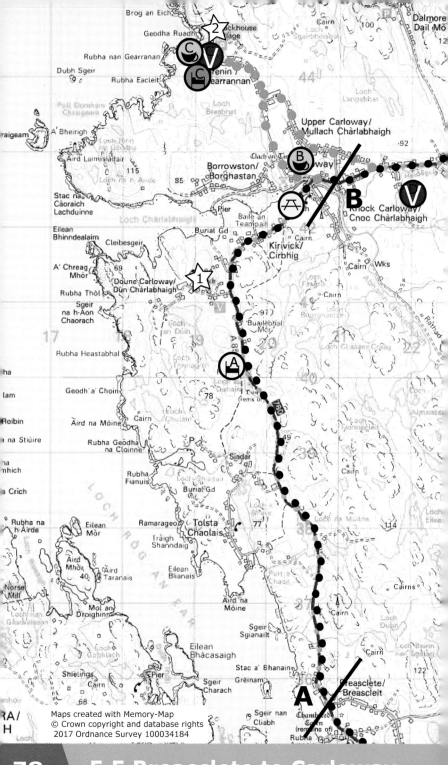

Maps created with Memory-Map
© Crown copyright and database rights
2017 Ordnance Survey 100034184

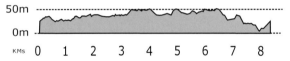

5.5 Breasclete to Carloway
Distance 8.3 km (5.2 miles)
Total ascent 128m
Total descent 128m

The Route

After leaving Breasclete with its BASF pharmaceutical factory (producing Omega-3 fatty acids), the Hebridean Way follows the A858 north through a low rock and lochan studded landscape. Pass by the turn for Carloway Broch and head on to cross the river in Carloway township.

Points of Interest

 Carloway Broch

Signposted, a short distance down a minor road. Brochs are Iron Age drystone structures found throughout Northern Scotland. Their purpose is still unclear: were they defensive structures, perhaps built as a response to slaving raids, or policing strongpoints or displays of wealth? Carloway is one of the best examples, standing on a rock outcrop overlooking a sea loch. Over 9m high in places, it shows how the hollow walls contained cells linked by staircases. There is a small visitor centre. Entrance to the site is free.

 Garenin Blackhouse Village

Signposted, a mile or so off the A road. Several blackhouses have been renovated: there is a museum, an exhibition about village life, a hostel, cafe and self-catering cottages. The houses were lived in until 1974, when the remaining residents moved to nearby council houses. The buildings, mostly thatched, are in a lovely setting above the bay and give a great idea of what the community must have looked like in the mid-20th century. The Arnol Blackhouse museum is perhaps a better example of a house from an earlier time. More information: http://www.gearrannan.com/

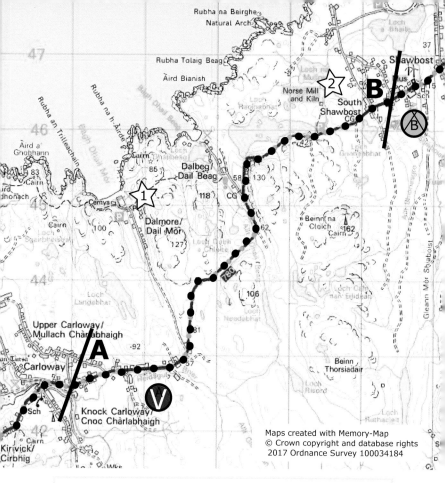

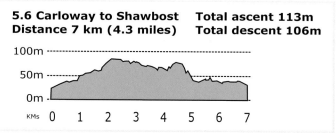

5.6 Carloway to Shawbost
Distance 7 km (4.3 miles) **Total ascent 113m**
Total descent 106m

The Route

Carry on along the A858, rising through Carloway to cross open moorland and run beneath low cliffs. After passing a long loch, descend gradually to the crofting township of Siabost, with its campsite, and school. The large building on the north side of the road is Siabost Harris Tweed Mill: it doesn't do tours!

Points of Interest

 Harris Tweed

Norman Mackenzie's weaving shed is just off the A road as you go up the hill in Carloway (signposted). He gives short demonstrations and sells scarfs, shawls and textile lengths (see listing 5.6.1). Nearby, on the road to Na Gearrannan, is the Carloway Tweed Mill (visits possible: www.thecarlowaymill.com 01851 643300).

1 Dalmore

Dail Mòr (or Dalmore) is reached by a turn to the left. The sandy beach, with rock stacks at the northeast end, is a favourite spot for surfers and photographers. In August 2016, an oil rig, the Transocean Winner, ran aground here as it was being towed from Norway to Malta. It was refloated after two weeks on the rocks, and towed round to Broad Bay on the east coast of the island. Whilst some pieces had broken off the rig, pollution appeared minimal.

2 Siabost Norse Mill and Kiln

A path leads over the hillside from a small car park by Loch Raoinebhat. Two buildings have been restored: a kiln for drying grain, and a water powered "Norse Mill" for grinding it. The thatched buildings were in regular use up until the 1920s: there is information about how the process and machinery worked. There were many such mills on the islands: place names containing Muilne are an indication.

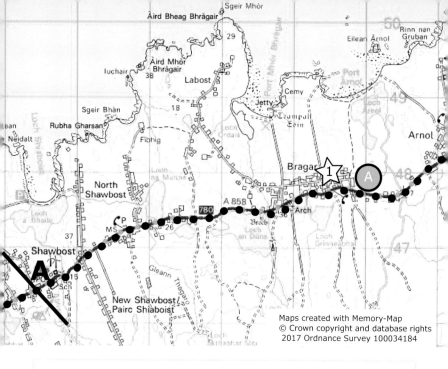

5.7 Shawbost to Barvas
Distance 11.1 km (6.9 miles)
Total ascent 123m
Total descent 145m

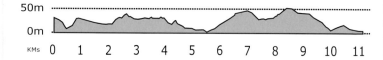

The Route

Carry straight along the A858. The road runs through Siabost, then over moorland past Loch an Duna (note the ruined dun on an island). Head through the crofting townships of Bragar and Arnol, before crossing more moorland leading to Loch Urrahag and its fishery. Cross another low hill and descend into the Barvas Glen. To the right, the hills of Beinn Bragar recede into the distance behind you. Increasingly, there is a feeling of heading onto open, flatter moorland. To the left there are snatched views of the sea and the coastline: these may beckon and encourage you to explore.

Maps created with Memory-Map
© Crown copyright and database rights
2017 Ordnance Survey 100034184

Points of Interest

 Bragar Whalebone Arch

On the north side of the road stands an intriguing arch formed from the jaws of a blue whale washed up at Bragar Bay in 1920. The whale lay rotting (imagine the stench!) for some time before the villagers were allowed to deal with it (and use it). The harpoon, which is part of the arch decoration, only exploded when it was being prepared for the exhibit. More information at: www.bragarwhalebone.co.uk

 Arnol Blackhouse

An Historic Scotland museum revolving around a restored, fully furnished blackhouse (Number 42), with accompanying exhibition. There is also a ruined blackhouse (Number 39) and the "whitehouse" that replaced it. Number 42 gives a good idea of what the many ruins you have passed along the way would have been like to live in: it was built around 1880 and lived in by people and their animals until 1966.

 Loch na Muilne

A small freshwater loch just a short walk beyond the Arnol Blackhouse. It is managed by the RSPB as red necked phalaropes, an unusual small wading bird, may be seen in the breeding season.

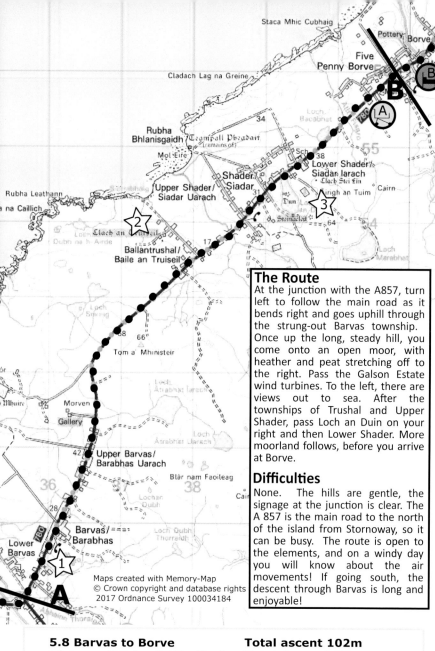

The Route

At the junction with the A857, turn left to follow the main road as it bends right and goes uphill through the strung-out Barvas township. Once up the long, steady hill, you come onto an open moor, with heather and peat stretching off to the right. Pass the Galson Estate wind turbines. To the left, there are views out to sea. After the townships of Trushal and Upper Shader, pass Loch an Duin on your right and then Lower Shader. More moorland follows, before you arrive at Borve.

Difficulties

None. The hills are gentle, the signage at the junction is clear. The A 857 is the main road to the north of the island from Stornoway, so it can be busy. The route is open to the elements, and on a windy day you will know about the air movements! If going south, the descent through Barvas is long and enjoyable!

Maps created with Memory-Map
© Crown copyright and database rights
2017 Ordnance Survey 100034184

5.8 Barvas to Borve
Distance 9.1 km (5.7 miles)

Total ascent 102m
Total descent 69m

50m
0m

KMs 0 1 2 3 4 5 6 7 8 9

Points of Interest

 ## Barvas

Loch Mor Barvas

Loch Mor Barvas dominates the landscape. On the east side a cairn marks the site of the last clan battle on the island between the Macaulays and Morrisons in 1654. According to local lore, it took place after a group of men from Clan Macaulay in Uig raided cattle from the Morrisons in Ness. The Macaulays were waylaid by the Morrisons in Barvas: many lives were lost. The surviving Macaulays were pursued as far as Uig where their leader, Zachary, was killed.

Barvas River

Martin Martin, writing in the late 17th century, records an ancient custom of sending a man to cross the Barvas River very early every May 1st. It was thought that if a female crossed first it would hinder the salmon from entering the river all year round. "They pretend to have learned this from a foreign sailor who was shipwrecked upon the coast a long time ago". Turn right at the junction in the village for the shop.

 ## Clach an Trushal

An impressive standing stone about half a mile towards the sea in Balantrushal. The monolith (5.8m high, 1.8m wide and nearly 1.5m thick) is claimed to be the largest standing stone in Europe. Some claim it marks the site of the last battle between the Morrisons and Macaulays, though it is thought to far predate this. Could it have been a sea mark?

 ## Steinacleit

Signposted as a stone circle above Loch an Duin (which plainly contains an island with a building on it), it is now thought that Steinacleit is not a stone circle, but the remains of a dwelling and walled enclosure or a robbed-out cairn. Either way, it is a pleasant place to visit and conjecture about whilst listening to the skylarks singing.

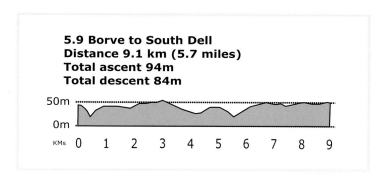

5.9 Borve to South Dell
Distance 9.1 km (5.7 miles)
Total ascent 94m
Total descent 84m

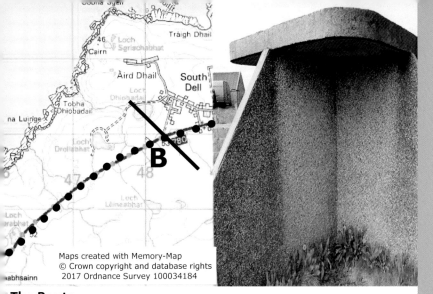

The Route

Descend through Borve: there is a shop and hotel on the right, and the pottery to your left. Carry on along the A587, climbing up from the river (look left at the old bridge) and across the moor. You pass the Galson Estate Community Business Centre on your right. At this point, if you are lucky, you may catch your first glimpse of the Butt of Lewis lighthouse (to the left of the road as you look down it). The end is in sight! Carry on along the A road past the Galson road ends, and climb up from the North Galson Burn. On a clear day the Butt of Lewis lighthouse is now easily seen.

Difficulties

The hills are not long or steep. Some summits are signed as "blind", as there is difficulty in looking over them. If the weather is against you, you will know about it and curse the wind.

Points of Interest

⟨1⟩ Galson Estate

The Galson Community Trust bought the 23,000 hectare estate in 2007: over 75% of the adult population of the crofting townships in the area are members. Amongst other projects, they run the Loch Stiapabhat nature reserve near the Butt, and have developed the wind energy project south of Ballantrushal. More information from: www.galsontrust.com

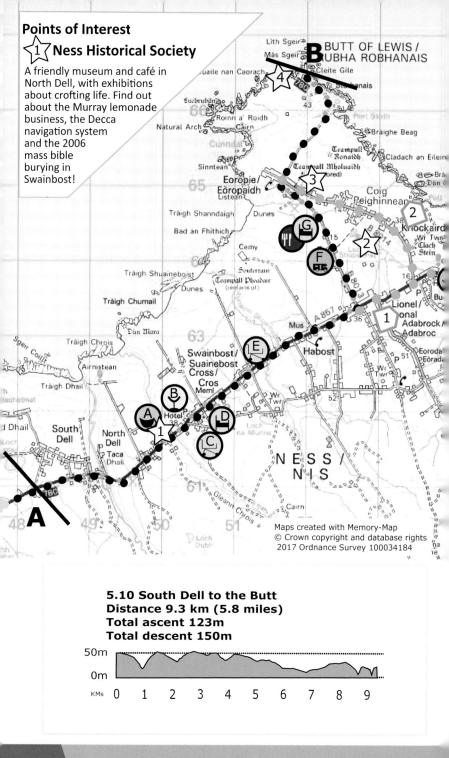

Points of Interest

☆1 Ness Historical Society

A friendly museum and café in North Dell, with exhibitions about crofting life. Find out about the Murray lemonade business, the Decca navigation system and the 2006 mass bible burying in Swainbost!

5.10 South Dell to the Butt
Distance 9.3 km (5.8 miles)
Total ascent 123m
Total descent 150m

Maps created with Memory-Map
© Crown copyright and database rights
2017 Ordnance Survey 100034184

The Route

Cross the Dell River to enter Ness and pass through the drawn-out townships of Dell, Cross, Swainbost, Habost and Lionel. Don't worry: it isn't obvious where one begins and another ends. At the junction with the B8013, turn left (the Hebridean Way signs here were obscured in March 2017).

Follow this road past the Decca Buttery on your left, and the school/ sports centre. Pass the left turn to the playpark and beach at Eoropie, and then curve around to the right. At the crossroads, go straight ahead on a minor road between wire fences enclosing long, thin, fields. Pass impressive lazy beds, cross a little burn leading to the beach of Port Sto (this is where to dip your toe in the sea, if you are that way inclined) and then curve to the left, following the coastline. Soon, the lighthouse comes into view. The metal Hebridean Way sign is just in front of the lighthouse.

Well done: you have cycled the Hebridean Way. Or at least read about finishing it!

Points of Interest

 ### Loch Stiapabhat

The Outer Hebrides' only Local Nature Reserve, it is an important stop-off and refuelling centre for birds migrating to or from Iceland and Greenland. Birds of prey are attracted by the other species. It is managed by the Galson Estate: a new hide, opened in 2014, has great views over the loch and nearby wetlands.

 ### Teampull Mholuaidh (St Moluag's Church)

Thought to date from the 12th century, and perhaps the earliest Christian site on Lewis. Restored in 1912, it is sometimes used by Stornoway's episcopal church. A strange side chapel is only connected to the nave by a low squint window. Martin Martin described the goings-on in the 17th century: "they all went to church and then standing silent for only a little time, one of them gave a signal…and immediately all of them went into the fields, where they fell a drinking their ale and spent the remainder of the night in dancing and singing, etc".

 ### The Butt of Lewis

The end of the road! All of Britain is behind you! On a still, sunny day it can be a marvellous place, in bad weather it is a truly awful one: it is reputed to be the windiest place in Britain. The lighthouse, with its brick tower, was built by the Stevensons in 1862 and automated in 1998. Watch the processions of gannets and gliding fulmar. See if you can see Cetaceans. But be careful! There is very little shelter. The coastline is exposed and the cliffs beyond the Butt are crumbling: there is a sad memorial to Angus Martin, who fell off in 1953.

Detours

 ### Port of Ness

A sandy beach and small fishing harbour with intricately winding quays and breakwaters. Prosperous from the pre-WWI Ling fishery, Ness is famous today for the guga hunters who harvest 2000 young gannets from Sula Sgeir each year. A centuries old tradition, it has a specific exemption from the 1954 Protection of Birds Act. The taste has been described as "akin to a rather tough goose that has been pickled in cod liver oil for at least a year".

 ### Dun Eistean

A small, atmospheric island reputed to be the original settlement of Clan Morrison. Archaeology projects have confirmed early mediaeval settlements, a tower and fortifications.

Facilities marked on our maps are in the full listings and summarised here.

Section 1 Vatersay and Barra

1.1.P
Shop with food, Bike Hire

Get on your Bike, Unit 1 Castlebay Development Estate, Castlebay, Isle of Barra

1.1.U
Bike Hire, Bike repair

Barra Bike Hire, Castlebay,

Section 2 Eriskay and South Uist

2.4.A
Bike Hire, Bike repair

Rothan Cycles, 9 Howmore, Isle of South Uist

Section 3 North Uist, Benbecula and Berneray

3.6.E
Bike Hire, Bike repair

Berneray Bikes, 13 Backhill, Berneray,

Section 4 Harris

4.1.H
Bed and Breakfast, Bike Hire

Sorrel Cottage, 2 Glen Kyles, Leverburgh, Isle of Harris

4.3.L
Shop with food, Bike Hire, Petrol Station

Ardhasaig Store and Filling Station, Ardhasaig, Isle of Harris

Other facilities for transport and repairs that might be useful are below

Bike Hire, Bike repair, Bike and people transport

Go Hebrides, Marvig, Isle of Lewis,LS2 9QP

01851 880320

www.gohebrides.com

john@gohebrides.com

Bike and people transport

Aldas Taxis, Lochmaddy, Isle of North Uist,HS6 5AD

01876 500215

Bike Hire, Bike repair

AD Cycle Centre, 67 Kenneth Street, Stornoway, Isle of Lewis,HS1 2DS

01851 704025

www.stornowaycycles.co.uk

info@stornowaycyclehire.co.uk

Bike Hire, Bike repair, Bike and people transport

Bike Hebrides, 6 Sand Street, Stornoway, Isle of Lewis,HS1 2UE

0777 594 3355

www.bikehebrides.com

jonnymurray@gmail.com

Bike Hire, Bike repair, Bike and people transport

BeSpoke Bicycles, Willowglen Road, Stornoway, Isle of Lewis,HS1 2EP

018510288264   0787 657 0932

http://bespoke-bicycle.com/

bespokebicyclerepairs@gmail.com

Section 1 Vatersay and Barra

1.1.A
Café

Macroons Tea Room, Pier Road, Castlebay, Isle of Barra, HS9 5XD

01871 810312
www.facebook.com/CastlebayPostOffice/

1.1.B
Café, Take away food, Restaurant

Café Kisimul, Main Street, Castlebay, Isle of Barra, HS9 5XD

01871 810 645
www.cafekisimul.co.uk
info@cafekisimul.co.uk

Morning till late

1.1.D
Tourist Information

Visit Scotland, Main Street, Castlebay, Isle of Barra, HS9 5XD

01871 810336
www.visitscotland.com/info/services/castlebay-icentre-p333281
castlebay@visitscotland.com

Summer Mon to Sat 9.15 to 16.45

1.1.E
Hotel, Restaurant, Pub/Inn/Bar

Craigard Hotel, Castlebay, Isle of Barra, HS9 5XD

01871 810200
www.craigardhotel.co.uk
craigardh@aol.com

1.1.F
Hotel, Restaurant

Castlebay Hotel, Castlebay, Isle of Barra, HS9 5XD

01871 810223
www.castlebay-hotel.co.uk
info@castlebayhotel.com

1.1.G
Shop with food

Buth Bharraigh, Castlebay, Isle of Barra, HS9 5UZ

01871 817948
www.barrahebrides.com/bth-bharraigh
info@buthbharraigh.co.uk

Mon to Sat 10.00 to 18.00, Sun 12.00 to 16.00

1.1.H
Bed and Breakfast

Tigh na Mara, Castlebay, Isle of Barra, HS9 5XD

01871 810304
www.tighnamara-barra.co.uk
linda@tighnamara-barra.co.uk

April to Oct

1.1.I
Café

The Deck, Hebridean Toffee, Castlebay Factory, Castlebay, Isle of Barra, HS9 5XD

01871 810898
www.hebrideantoffeecompany.com
hebtoffee@aol.com

1.1.J
Hostel

Dunard Hostel, Castlebay, Isle of Barra, HS9 5XD

01871 810443
www.dunardhostel.co.uk
info@dunardhostel.co.uk

1.1.K
Bed and Breakfast

Endeavour Bed and Breakfast, Castlebay, Isle of Barra, HS9 5UZ

01871 810757   07855 457283
www.isleofbarra.com/endeavour.htm
endeavourcastlebay@gmail.com

1.1.L
Bed and Breakfast

Grianamul Bed and Breakfast, Castlebay, Isle of Barra, HS9 5XD

01871 810416
www.isleofbarraaccommodation.com/bed__breakfast.html

ronniemacneil@live.com

1.1.M
Café, Visitor Centre/Museum

Dualchas Heritage Centre, Castlebay, Isle of Barra, HS9 5DX

01871 810413
www.barraheritage.com/dualchas

1.1.N
Café

Tartan Table Café, Barra Children's Centre, Castlebay, Isle of Barra, HS9 5XD

07497 312168
www.facebook.com/Tartan-Table-Cafe-265201166849521

tartantable@btinternet.com

Mon to Sat 10.00 to 15.30

1.1.O
Shop with food

The Co-operative, Castlebay, Isle of Barra, HS9 5DX

01871 810069
www.co-operative.coop/store/food/HS9-5XD/isle-of-barra

Mon to Sat 7.00 to 22.00, Sun 12.30 to 22.00

1.1.P
Shop with food, Bike Hire

Get on your Bike, Unit 1 Castlebay Development Estate, Castlebay, Isle of Barra, HS9 5XF

01871 810846   07908 267265
www.croft183.com/barra-bike-hire/

barraholidays@gmail.com

Mon to Sat 9.00 to 18.00, Sun 12.30 to 17.00

1.1.Q
Bed and Breakfast

Bayview Guest House, Nask, Isle of Barra, HS9 5XN

01871 810511
www.barra-bayview.co.uk

info@barra-bayview.co.uk

1.1.R
Take away food

Barra Pizza, 63 Tangasdale, Kinloch, Isle of Barra, HS9 5XW

01871 241 699
www.barrapizza.co.uk/

info@barrapizza.co.uk

Fri to Sat 17.00 to 20.00

1.1.S
Hotel

The Isle of Barra Beach Hotel, Tangasdale, Isle of Barra, HS9 5XW

01871 810383
www.isleofbarrahotel.co.uk

barrahotel@aol.com

1.1.T
Camping with facilities

Barra Camping, 104a Borve, Isle of Barra, HS9 5XR

01871 810878   0753 0265531
www.barracamping.co.uk/

donald@barracamping.co.uk

1.1.U
Bike Hire, Bike repair

Barra Bike Hire, Castlebay,

07876 402842
www.barrabikehire.co.uk

info@barrabikehire.co.uk

1.2.A
Hotel, Restaurant, Pub/Inn/Bar

Heathbank Hotel, Northbay, Isle of Barra, HS9 5YQ

01871 890266
www.barrahotel.co.uk
info@barrahotel.co.uk

1.2.B
Café

Barra Airport Café, Barra Airport, Eoligarry, Isle of Barra, HS9 5YD

07855 143545
www.facebook.com/barraairportcafe

Every day 10.00 to 16.00 (summer) 15.00 (winter)

1.2.C
Camping with facilities

Scuribhal Campsite, 10 Eoligarry, Northbay, Isle of Barra, HS9 5YD

01871 890292   07896 471580

1.2.D
Camping with facilities

Croft No2, Scurrival Point, 2 Eoligarry, Isle of Barra, HS9 5YD

01871 890327   07772 487169
http://www.barracampsite.com/
info@barracampsite.com

1.2.E
Bed and Breakfast

Sealladh Na Mara, 11A Ardmhor, Isle of Barra, HS9 5YB

01871 890743
www.bedinbarra.com
lornareckord@aol.com

Section 2 Eriskay and South Uist

2.1.A
Café, Shop with food

Eriskay Shop, Rudha Ban, Isle of Eriskay, HS8 5JJ

01878 720236
www.facebook.com/butheirisgeidh
eriskayshop@gmail.com

Mon to Sat 09.00 to 18.00

2.1.B
Pub/Inn/Bar

Am Politician, Isle of Eriskay, HS8 5JL

01878 720246
www.facebook.com/pages/Politician/66
5235940191522

2.1.C
Bed and Breakfast

Oir na Mara, 5b Baile, Isle of Eriskay, HS8 5LJ

01878 720216
macinnes5b@hotmail.co.uk

2.1.D
Bed and Breakfast

An Taigh Mor, 15b Balla, Eriskay, Isle of South Uist, HS8 5JL

01878 720717
https://antaighmor.com/
antaighmorbandb@gmail.com

2.2.A
Café, Camping with facilities

Kilbride Campsite, West Kilbride, West Kilbride, Isle of South Uist, HS8 5TT

01878 700568   07751 251522
www.kilbridecampsite.co.uk
mailbox@kilbridecampsite.co.uk

Café- Mon to Sat 9.00 to 17.00, Sun 12.00 to 16.00

2.2.B
Hotel, Restaurant, Pub/Inn/Bar

Polochar Inn, Polachar, Isle of South Uist, HS8 5TT

01878 700215
www.polocharinn.com/

polocharinn@aol.com

2.2.C
Bed and Breakfast

Ard Na Mara, Kilpheder, Isle of South Uist, HS8 5TB

01878 700452
www.ardnamara.co.uk

info@ardnamara.co.uk

2.2.D
Hotel

The Borrodale Hotel, Daliburgh, Isle of South Uist, HS8 5SS

01878 700444
www.isleshotelgroup.co.uk

reception@borrodalehotel.co.uk

2.2.E
Shop with food

The Co-operative, 292 Daliburgh, Isle of South Uist, HS8 5SS

01878 700326
www.coop.co.uk/store/food/HS8-5SS/292-daliburgh

Mon to Sat 7.00 to 22.00, Sun 12.30 to 22.00

2.2.F
Bed and Breakfast

Karingeidha, Daliburgh, Isle of South Uist, HS8 5SS

01878 700495
karingeidha@hotmail.com

2.3.A
Bed and Breakfast

Kilvale Bed and Breakfast, 240 Garrhellie, Isle of South Uist, HS8 5SX

01878 700394   07851 190928
www.kilvale.com

maggie_steele@hotmail.com

2.3.B
Café, Visitor Centre/Museum

Kildonan Museum, Kildonan, Isle of South Uist, HS8 5RZ

01878 710343
www.kildonanmuseum.co.uk

admin@kildonanmuseum.co.uk

April to Oct Mon to Sun 10.00 to 17.00

2.3.C
Bed and Breakfast

Invercanny, Garryhallie, Isle of South Uist, HS8 5SX

01878 700894   07723 219813
www.facebook.com/Invercanny-BB-South-Uist-Western-Isles-521703021346150/?nr

2.4.A
Bike Hire, Bike repair

Rothan Cycles, 9 Howmore, Isle of South Uist, HS8 5SH

01870 620286
www.rothan.scot

2.4.B
Hostel, Camping using hostel facilities

The Gatliff Trust, Howmore, Isle of South Uist, HS8 5SH

www.gatliff.org.uk

2.5.A
Café

Hebridean Jewellery, Iochdar, Isle of South Uist, HS8 5QX

01870 610288
www.hebrideanjewellery.co.uk

info@hebridean-jewellery.co.uk

2.5.B
Shop with food

Lovats Supermarket, Carnan, Isle of South Uist, HS8 5QX

01870 610340

Section 3 North Uist, Benbecula and Berneray

3.1.A
Shop with food

The Co-operative, Creagorry, Isle of Benbecula, HS7 5PG

01870 602231
www.coop.co.uk/store/food/HS7-5PG/creagorry

Mon to Sat 7.00 to 22.00, Sun 12.30 to 22.00

3.1.B
Hotel

Isle of Benbecula House Hotel, Creagorry, Isle of Benbecula, HS7 5PG

01870 603046
www.isleshotelgroup.co.uk

iobhotel.reservations@isleshotelgroup.co.uk

3.1.C
Bed and Breakfast

Bainbhidh, Liniclate, Isle of Benbecula, HS7 5PY

01870 602532
mruadh@gmail.com

3.1.D
Bed and Breakfast

Orcadia, Liniclate, Isle of Benbecula, HS7 5PJ

01870 602014
freda.henderson@ymail.com

3.1.E
Bed and Breakfast

Hestimul, 21 Lionacleit, Liniclate, Isle of Benbecula, HS7 5PJ

01870 602033

3.1.F
Hotel

Dark Island Hotel, Liniclate, Isle of Benbecula, HS7 5PJ

01870 603030
http://darkislandhotel.co.uk/

reservations@darkislandhotel.co.uk

3.1.G
Hotel, Camping with facilities

Shell Bay House and Caravan Park, Liniclate, Isle of Benbecula, HS7 5PJ

01870 602447
shellbaylin@aol.com

3.1.H
Bed and Breakfast

Borve Guest House, 5 Torlum, Isle of Benbecula, HS7 5PP

01870 602685   07818 203373
www.borveguesthouse.com

info@borveguesthouse.com

3.1.I
Hostel

Nunton House, Nunton, Isle of Benbecula, HS7 5LU

01870 602017   07786 158304
www.nuntonhousehostel.com

nuntonhousehostel@hotmail.co.uk

3.1.J
Café, Gallery

Nunton Steadings, Nunton, Isle of Benbecula, HS7 5LU

01870 603774
https://www.facebook.com/nuntonsteadingsbenbecula/

nuntonsteadings@gmail.com

Summer opening only

3.1.K
Bed and Breakfast

5 Nunton, Nunton, Isle of Benbecula, HS7 5LU

01870 603463

http://5nunton.uk/

bookings@5nunton.uk

3.1.L
Shop with food

Maclennans Supermarket, 2 Balivanich, Isle of Benbecula, HS7 5LA

01870 602308

www.maclennanssupermarket.co.uk

info@maclennanssupermarket.co.uk

Mon to Sat 8.00 to 20.00, Sun 11.00 to 16.00

3.1.M
Restaurant

Stepping Stones Restaurant, Balivanich, Isle of Benbecula, HS7 5LA

01870 603377

www.facebook.com/TheSteppingStoneRestaurant/

enquiries@macleansbakery.co.uk

Check website

3.1.N
Gallery, Shop with food

Macgillvary and Co, Balivanich, Isle of Benbecula, HS7 5LA

01870 602525

www.macgil.co.uk

info@m-ff.co.uk

3.1.P
Bed and Breakfast

Ceann na Pairc Guest House, 3 Nunton, Isle of Benbecula, HS7 5LU

01870 602017   07825 233050

www.ceann-na-pairc.com

ceann-na-pairc@hotmail.co.uk

3.2.A
Bakery

Macleans Bakery, Uachdar Balivanich, Isle of Benbecula, HS7 5LY

01870 602659

macleanbakery@btconnect.com

Mon to Fri 8.00 to 15.00, Sat 8.00 to 14.00

3.2.B
Hostel, Camping with facilities, Camping pods/glamping

Moorcroft Holidays, 17 Carinish, Isle of North Uist, HS6 5HN

01876 580305

www.moorcroftholidays.co.uk

morrisons17@hotmail.com

April to Oct

3.3.A
Hotel, Restaurant

Temple View Hotel, Isle of North Uist, HS6 5EJ

01876 580676

www.templeviewhotel.co.uk

templeviewhotel@aol.com

3.3.B
Bed and Breakfast

Bonnie View, 19 Carinish, Isle of North Uist, HS6 5HN

01876 580211

heather@carinish.wanadoo.co.uk

3.3.C
Bed and Breakfast

The Ships Wheel, 23b Claddach Baleshore, Isle of North Uist, HS6 5EN

01876 580785

www.theshipswheel.co.uk

calumandpat@gmail.com

3.3.D
Shop with food

The Hebridean Smokehouse, Clachan, Isle of North Uist, HS6 5HD

01876 580209
www.hebrideansmokehouse.com

sales@hebrideansmokehouse.com

Mon to Fri 8.00 to 17.30, Sat (Easter to Oct) 9.00 to 17.00

3.3.E
Café

Claddach Kirkibost Café, Isle of North Uist, HS6 5EP

01876 580390
www.claddach-kirkibost.org/our-cafe

sales@hebrideankitchen.com

Mon to fri 9.00 to 17.00, Sat 11.00 to 16.00, Sun 11.00 to 15.00 (summer only)

3.3.F
Pub/Inn/Bar

Westford Inn, Claddach Kirkibost, Isle of North Uist, HS6 5EP

01876 580653
www.facebook.com/WestfordInn

westfordinn@hotmail.com

3.3.G
Shop with food

Bayhead Shop, 5 Sollas, Bayhead, Isle of North Uist, HS6 5DS

01876 510257
www.facebook.com/bayheadshop/

Mon to Sat 8.00 to 18.00

3.3.H
Bed and Breakfast

The Old Shop House, Bayhead, Isle of North Uist, HS6 5DS

01876 510395
theoldshophouse.com

morag@theoldshophouse.co.uk

3.3.I
Hostel, Camping with facilities, Camping pods/glamping

The Tractor Shed, Paible, Isle of North Uist, HS6 5DZ

07952 163080
www.northuistbunkhouse.co.uk

info@northuistbunkhouse.co.uk

3.4.A
Camping with facilities

Balranald Campsite, Hougharry, Isle of North Uist, HS6 5DL

01876 510304   07748 267996
www.balranaldhebrideanholidays.com

info@balranaldhebrideanholidays.com

3.5.A
Bed and Breakfast

Struan House, 12 Malaglate, Sollas, Isle of North Uist, HS6 5BX

01876 560385   07818 615742
www.struanhousesollas.co.uk

shonnieshep@hotmail.com

3.5.B
Bed and Breakfast

The Rowan Tree, 4b Middlequarter, Sollas, Isle of North Uist, HS6 5BU

01876 560445   07525 186575
www.therowantree.co.uk

enquiries@therowantree.co.uk

3.5.C
Shop with food

The Co-operative, Sollas, Isle of North Uist, HS6 5BS

01876 560210
https://finder.coop.co.uk/food/store/HS6-5BS/sollas

Mon to Sat 7.00 to 22.00

3.5.D
Bed and Breakfast

Bed and Breakfast, 4A Ahmore, Isle of North Uist, HS6 5BW

01876 560425
mabrit53@yahoo.co.uk

3.5.E
Bed and Breakfast

Sheillaidh, 8 Sollas, Isle of North Uist, HS6 5BS

01876 560332
menziesfm@aol.com

3.6.A
Café, Shop with food

Ardmaree Stores and Lobster Pot Tea Room, 5a Borve, Berneray, HS6 5BJ

01876 540288
www.ardmareestores.co.uk

ardmaree.lobsterpot@yahoo.co.uk

Mon-Sat- summer 9.00 to 18.00, winter 9.00 to 17.30

3.6.B
Bed and Breakfast

Seal View, 16 Backhill, Berneray, HS6 5BD

01876 540209
www.sealview.com

andrew@sealview.com

3.6.C
Hostel, Camping using hostel facilities

The Gatliff Trust, Berneray, HS6 5BQ

www.gatliff.org.uk

3.6.D
Bed and Breakfast, Café

Tir nan Og, Sandhill, Berneray, HS6 5BQ

01876 540333
tirnanogberneray@btinternet.com

3.6.E
Bike Hire, Bike repair

Berneray Bikes, 13 Backhill, Berneray, HS6 5BD

07340 175276
www.berneraybikes.co.uk

berneraybikes@hotmail.com

Section 4 Harris

4.1.A
Restaurant

The Anchorage Restaurant, The Pier, Leverburgh, Isle of Harris, HS5 3UB

01859 520 225
Mon to Sat 12.00 to 22.00 (last orders 21.00). Sunday 12.30 to 15.30

4.1.B
Take away food

The Butty Bus, Leverburgh, Isle of Harris, HS5 3UF

07899 786574

4.1.D
Hostel

Am Bothan Bunk House, Ferry Road, Leverburgh, Isle of Harris, HS5 3UA

01859 520251
www.ambothan.com

info@ambothan.com

4.1.E
Bed and Breakfast

Ben View, Leverburgh, Isle of Harris, HS5 3TL

01859 520316
www.bedbreakfastharris.co.uk

benview.leverburgh@outlook.com

4.1.F
Shop with food

Harris Community Co-op, Leverburgh, Isle of Harris,

01859 520370
www.harriscommunityshop.co.uk

sales@harriscommunityshop.co.uk

Mon to Thu 9.00 to 18.00 Fri and Sat 9.00 to 19.00

4.1.G
Bed and Breakfast

Taylor Hill Bed and Breakfast, Leverburgh, Isle of Harris,

01859 520266
www.taylorhill.co

bookings@taylorhill.co

4.1.H
Bed and Breakfast, Bike Hire

Sorrel Cottage, 2 Glen Kyles, Leverburgh, Isle of Harris, HS5 3TY

01859 520319
www.accommodationisleofharris.co.uk

sorrel.cottage@virgin.net

4.1.I
Take away food

Croft 36, Northton, Isle of Harris, HS3 3JA

01859 520779   07500 341888
www.croft36.com

croft36northton@yahoo.co.uk

Mon to Fri

4.1.J
Café

The Temple Café, Magillivary Centre, Northton, Isle of Harris, HS3 3JA

07876 340416
www.facebook.com/TheTempleCafe?_rdr

Tues-Sun 10.30 to 17.00. Evening meals Thurs, Fri, Sun

4.1.K
Café, Visitor Centre/Museum

Seallam! Visitor Centre, Northton, Isle of Harris, HS3 3JA

01859 520258
www.hebridespeople.com

info@hebridespeople.com

Mon-Sat 10 to 17.00 through summer

4.1.L
Hotel, Restaurant

Scarista House, Sgarasta Bheag, Isle of Harris, HS3 3HX

01859 550238
www.scaristahouse.com

bookings@scaristahouse.com

4.1.M
Bed and Breakfast

Sandview House, 6 Scaristavore, Isle of Harris, HS3 3HX

01859 550212
sandviewhouse@gmail.com

4.2.A
Bed and Breakfast, Restaurant

Pairc an t-Srath, Borve, Isle of Harris, HS3 3HT

01859 550386
www.paircant-srath.co.uk

info@paircant-srath.co.uk

4.2.C
Bed and Breakfast

Horgabost Bed and Breakfast, 1 Horgabost, Isle of Harris, HS3 3HR

01859 550285
www.agnesmaclennan.co.uk

4.2.D
Camping with facilities

Horgabost Campsite, Isle of Harris, HS3 3HR

01859 550386

4.2.E
Bed and Breakfast

Beul na Mara, 12 Seilebost, Isle of Harris, HS3 3HP

01859 550205   07769 923568
www.beulnamara.co.uk

4.2.G
Bed and Breakfast

Luskentyre Lodge, 3 Luskentyre, Isle of Harris, HS3 3HL

01859 550259
www.isleofharris.co

stay@isleofharris.co

4.2.H
Café, Motorhome parking

West Harris Trust, Talla Na Mara, Pairc Niseaboist, Isle of Harris, HS3 3AE

01859 503901
www.westharristrust.org

admin@westharristrust.org

4.2.I
Motorhome parking

West Harris Trust, Seilebost, Isle of Harris,

01859 550457
www.westharristrust.org

admin@westharristrust.org

4.2.J
Motorhome parking

West Harris Trust, On the road to Tarbert, Sgarasta Mhor, Isle of Harris,

01859 550457
www.westharristrust.org

admin@westharristrust.org

4.3.A
Camping with facilities

Minch View Touring Park, 10 Drinishader, Isle of Harris, HS3 3DX

01859 511207
https://minchview.wordpress.com/

4.3.B
Bed and Breakfast

Rodean, Kendibig, Isle of Harris, HS3 3HQ

01859 502079
famorrison@hotmail.co.uk

4.3.C
Bed and Breakfast

Ceol na Mara, 7 Direcleit, Isle of Harris, HS3 3DP

01859 502464
www.ceolnamara.com

4.3.D
Café, Visitor Centre/Museum

Isle of Harris Distillery, Tarbert, Isle of Harris, HS3 3DJ

01859 502212
www.harrisdistillery.com

info@harrisdistillery.com

4.3.E
Hostel

Backpackers Stop, Main Street, Tarbert, Isle of Harris, HS3 3DJ

01859 502163   07708 746745
www.backpackers-stop.co.uk/

bpackers_stop@hotmail.com

4.3.F
Café, Shop with food, Take away food

Various shops in Tarbert, Isle of Harris,

4.3.G
Hotel, Restaurant, Pub/Inn/Bar

Hotel Hebrides, Pier Road, Tarbert, Isle of Harris, HS3 3DG

01859 502364
www.hotel-hebrides.com

stay@hotel-hebrides.com

4.3.H
Tourist Information

Visit Scotland, Tarbert iCentre, Pier Road, Isle of Harris, HS3 3DG

01859 502011
www.visitscotland.com/info/services/tarbert-information-centre-p333311
TarbertHarris@visitscotland.com

Mon-Sat possibly only during summer

4.3.I
Hotel, Restaurant, Pub/Inn/Bar

Harris Hotel, Tarbert, Isle of Harris, HS3 3DL

01859 502154
www.harrishotel.com
info@harrishotel.com

4.3.J
Bed and Breakfast

Avalon Guest House, 12 West Side, West Tarbert, Isle of Harris, HS3 3BG

01859 502334
www.avalonguesthouse.org
arlenemorrison2334@hotmail.com

4.3.K
Café, Gallery

Hebscape, Ardhasaig, Isle of Harris, HS3 3AJ

01859 502363
www.hebscapegallery.co.uk
info@hebscapegallery.co.uk
Tues-Sat 11.00 to 17.30

4.3.L
Shop with food, Bike Hire, Petrol Station

Ardhasaig Store and Filling Station, Ardhasaig, Isle of Harris, HS3 3AJ

01859 502066

4.3.M
Hotel, Restaurant

Ardhasaig House, Ardhasaig, Isle of Harris, HS3 3AJ

01859 502500   07765 211375
www.ardhasaig.co.uk
info@ardhasaig.co.uk

4.4.A
Bed and Breakfast

Seaforth, Ardvourlie, Isle of Harris, HS3 3AB

01859 502031   07470086749
ardvourliebandb.co.uk
croftercampbell@btinternet.com

4.4.B
Hostel

Scaladale Centre, Ardvourlie, Isle of Harris, HS3 3AB

01859 502502
www.scaladale-centre.co.uk
info@scaladale.co.uk

4.4.C
Hostel, Camping using hostel facilities

The Gatliff Trust, Rhenigdale, Isle of Harris, HS3 3BD

www.gatliff.org.uk

Section 5 Lewis

5.2.A
Bed and Breakfast

Lochside Bed and Breakfast, Lochside, 54 Balallan, Isle of Lewis, HS2 9PT

07944 617 562
Joeblakey123@gmail.com

5.2.B
Bed and Breakfast

Clearview Bed and Breakfast, Balallan, Isle of Lewis, HS2 9PT

01851 830472
www.clearview-lewis.co.uk
stay@clearview-lewis.co.uk

Section 5 Lewis

5.2.C
Visitor Centre/Museum

Kinloch Historical Society, Old School, Balallan, Isle of Lewis, HS2 9LA

01851 830778
https://www.facebook.com/Kinloch-Historical-Society-556752561063329/
kinlochhistorical@hotmail.co.uk

5.2.D
Restaurant, Pub/Inn/Bar

Loch Erisort Inn, Sheildinish, Isle of Lewis, HS2 9RA

01851 830473
www.locherisortinn.co.uk
info@locherisortinn.co.uk

5.2.E
Bed and Breakfast, Café, Gallery

Tigh na Bruaich, 8 Balallan, Lochs, Isle of Lewis, HS2 9PN

01851 830742   07760 245405
www.saa.co.uk/art/islandarts
tighnabruaich@tiscali.co.uk
Mon-Sat 10.00 to 18.00

5.2.F
Bed and Breakfast

Gledfield Bed and Breakfast, 5 Balallan, Isle of Lewis, HS2 9PN

01851 830233
www.gledfield-balallan.co.uk

5.2.G
Bed and Breakfast

Benlester, 13 Habost, South Lochs, Isle of Lewis, HS2 9QB

01851 880767
www.benlester.net
mary@benlester.net

5.2.H
Bed and Breakfast

Taigh Chailean, 11 Laxay, Lacasaigh, Isle of Lewis, HS2 9PJ

01851 830315   07557 735399
www.lewisbedbreakfast.co.uk
info@lewisbedbreakfast.co.uk

5.2.J
Hostel, Café, Shop with food, Bird of Prey Trail, Visitor Centre/Museum, Bike Hire

Ravenspoint, Kershader, Isle of Lewis, HS2 9QA

01851 880236
ravenspoint.net
hostel@ravenspoint.net

5.3.A
Café, Shop with food, Petrol Station

Lochs Services, Leurbost, Isle of Lewis, HS2 9PE

01851 860377

5.3.B
Motorhome parking

Loch View, Isle of Lewis,

07760 151729   07920 000356

5.3.C
Bed and Breakfast

Westend, 16b Achmore, Isle of Lewis,

01851 860204   0755 466 5549
www.magaidhsmith.co.uk
maggiesmith@hebrides.net

5.3.D
Bed and Breakfast

Ghinda, 1a Lochganvich, Isle of Lewis, HS2 9DT

01851 860333
www.ghinda1a.co.uk
ghinda1a@hebrides.net

5.4.A
Bed and Breakfast

Creagan B & B, Callanish, Isle of Lewis, HS2 9DY

01851 621200   07766 942637
www.creagan-bedandbreakfast.co.uk

ann@creagan-bedandbreakfast.co.uk

5.4.B
Café, Visitor Centre/Museum, Shop- not food

Calanais Visitor Centre, Isle of Lewis, HS2 9DY

01851 621422
www.callanishvisitorcentre.co.uk

callanishfarmtrust@gmail.com

Mon-Sat 10.00 to 18.00

5.4.C
Camping pods/glamping

Calanais Camping, Isle of Lewis, HS2 9DY

07809 330971
www.callanishcamping.co.uk

5.4.E
Bed and Breakfast

Loch Roag Guest House, 22a Breasclete, Isle of Lewis, HS2 9EF

01851 621771
http://lochroag.com/

info@lochroag.com

5.5.A
Hotel, Restaurant

Doune Braes Hotel, Carloway, Isle of Lewis, HS2 9AA

01851 643252
www.doune-braes.co.uk

hebrides@doune-braes.co.uk

5.5.B
Café, Gallery

Blue Pig Studio, 11 Upper Carloway, Isle of Lewis, HS2 9AG

01851 643225
www.janeharlington.co.uk

bluepigstudio@googlemail.com

5.5.C
Hostel, Café, Visitor Centre/Museum

Na Gearrannan Blackhouse Village, Carloway, Isle of Lewis, HS2 9AL

01851 643416
www.gearrannan.com

info@gearrannan.com

April to September, Mon-Sat 9.30 to 17.30

5.6.A
Shop- not food

Carloway Harris Tweeds, Park House, Carloway, Isle of Lewis, HS2 9AH

01851 643416
www.carlowayharristweed.com

info@carlowayharristweed.co.uk

Generally open if Norman is there

5.6.B
Camping with facilities

Eilean Fraoich, North Shawbost, Isle of Lewis, HS2 9BQ

01851 710504
www.eileanfraoich.co.uk

5.7.A
Café, Take away food, Restaurant

40 North Foods, 40 North Bragar, Isle of Lewis, HS2 9DA

01851 710424
www.40northfoods.co.uk

bruce.armitage@40north.co.uk

Tues-Sat 12.00 to 19.00 (take away), later opening for restaurant

5.7.B
Shop with food, Petrol Station

Welcome Inn, Lower Barvas, Isle of Lewis, HS2 0RA

01851 840343

5.8.A
Shop with food, Petrol Station

Borve Mini Market, Borve, Isle of Lewis, HS2 0RX

01851 850410
myweb.tiscali.co.uk/borveminimarket
borveminimarket@tiscali.co.uk

Mon-Sat 8.00 to 20.00

5.8.B
Hotel, Restaurant

Borve Country House Hotel, Borve, Isle of Lewis, HS2 0RX

01851 850223 07887 607777
www.borvehousehotel.co.uk

info@borvehousehotel.co.uk

5.9.A
Hostel, Bed and Breakfast

Galson Farm Guest House, South Galson, Isle of Lewis, HS2 0SH

01851 850492
http://www.galsonfarm.co.uk/

galsonfarm@yahoo.com

5.9.B
Bed and Breakfast

Heather View, 55 Heatherview, North Glaston, Isle of Lewis, HS2 0SJ

01851 850471
http://heatherviewisleoflewis.co.uk

heatherview@icloud.com

5.10.A
Café, Visitor Centre/Museum

Ness Historical Society, Cross School, Ness, Isle of Lewis, HS2 0SN

01851 810377
http://eachdraidhnis.org

office@cenonline.org

5.10.B
Pub/Inn/Bar

The Cross Inn, Ness, Lewis, HS2 0SN

01851 810152
www.crossinn.com

info@crossinn.com

5.10.C
Shop with food

Cross Stores, 7 Cross Skigersta Road, Ness, Isle of Lewis, HS2 0TD

01851 810241
www.facebook.com/crossstores/

Mon-Fri 9.00 to 18.00, Sat 9.00 to 19.00

5.10.D
Bed and Breakfast

Cabuzana, Back Street, Cross, Isle of Lewis, HS2 0SY

01851 810154
www.cabuzanabandb.com

annie.mack@live.co.uk

5.10.E
Shop with food, Petrol Station

Swainbost Shop, 28 Swainbost, Ness, Isle of Lewis, HS2 0TA

01851 810223

5.10.F
Motorhome parking

Sporsnis, Lionel, Port of Ness, Isle of Lewis, HS2 0XB

01851 810039
www.sporsnis.co.uk/

info@sporsnis.co.uk

5.10.G
Bed and Breakfast, Restaurant

The Decca, Lionel, Ness, Isle of Lewis, HS2 0XB

01851 810571
www.thedecca.co.uk

louise@thedecca.co.uk

5.10.H
Café, Restaurant

Cafe Sonas, Port of Ness, Isle of Lewis, HS2 0XA

01851 810222
https://www.facebook.com/Cafe-Sonas-at-Port-of-Ness-Beach-and-Harbour-369978956368578/

magaidh1@aol.com

INDEX